Meeting Customer Needs

Meeting Customer Needs

Second edition

Ian Smith

*Published in association with
the Institute of Management*

Butterworth-Heinemann
Linacre House, Jordan Hill, Oxford OX2 8DP
225 Wildwood Avenue, Woburn, MA 01801-2041
A division of Reed Educational and Professional Publishing Ltd

R̵ A member of the Reed Elsevier plc group

OXFORD   BOSTON   JOHANNESBURG
MELBOURNE   NEW DELHI   SINGAPORE

First published 1994
Reprinted 1994, 1995
Second edition 1997
Reprinted 1998

© Reed Educational and Professional Publishing Ltd 1997

British Library Cataloguing in Publication Data
A catalogue record for this book is available from the British Library

ISBN 0 7506 3391 3

Composition by Genesis Typesetting, Laser Quay, Rochester, Kent
Printed and bound in Great Britain by
Biddles Ltd, Guildford and King's Lynn

PLANT A TREE

BTCV
*British Trust for
Conservation Volunteers*

FOR EVERY TITLE THAT WE PUBLISH, BUTTERWORTH-HEINEMANN
WILL PAY FOR BTCV TO PLANT AND CARE FOR A TREE.

Contents

Series adviser's preface

This books is one of a series designed for people wanting to develop their capabilities as managers. You might think that there isn't anything very new in that. In one way you would be right. The fact that very many people want to learn to become better managers is not new, and for many years a wide range of approaches to such learning and development has been available. These have included courses leading to formal qualifications, organizationally based management development programmes and a whole variety of self-study materials. A copious literature, extending from academic textbooks to sometimes idiosyncratic prescriptions from successful managers and consultants, has existed to aid – or perhaps confuse – the potential seeker after managerial truth and enlightenment.

So what is new about this series? In fact, a great deal – marking in some ways a revolution in our thinking both about the art of managing and also the process of developing managers.

Where did it all begin? Like most revolutions, although there may be a single, identifiable act that precipitated the uprising, the roots of discontent are many and long established. The debate about the performance of British managers, the way managers are educated and trained, and the extent to which shortcomings in both these areas have contributed to our economic decline, has been running for several decades.

Until recently, this debate had been marked by periods of frenetic activity – stimulated by some report or enquiry and perhaps ending in some new initiatives or policy changes – followed by relatively long periods of comparative calm. But the underlying causes for concern persisted. Basically, the majority of managers in the UK appeared to have little or no training for their role, certainly far less than their counterparts in our major competitor nations. And there was concern about the nature, style and appropriateness of the management education and training that was available.

The catalyst for this latest revolution came in late 1986 and early 1987, when three major reports reopened the whole issue. The 1987 reports were *The Making of British Managers* by John Constable and Roger McCormick, carried out for the British Institute of Management and the CBI, and *The Making of*

Managers by Charles Handy, carried out for the (then) Manpower Services Commission, National Economic Development Office and British Institute of Management. The 1986 report, which often receives less recognition than it deserves as a key contribution to the recent changes, was *Management Training: context and process* by Iain Mangham and Mick Silver, carried out for the Economic and Social Research Council and the Department of Trade and Industry.

This is not the place to review in detail what the reports said. Indeed, they and their consequences are discussed in several places in this series of books. But essentially they confirmed that:

- British managers were undertrained by comparison with their counterparts internationally.
- The majority of employers invested far too little in training and developing their managers.
- Many employers found it difficult to specify with any degree of detail just what it was that they required successful managers to be able to do.

The Constable/McCormick and Handy reports advanced various recommendations for addressing these problems, involving an expansion of management education and development, a reformed structure of qualifications and a commitment from employers to a code of practice for management development. While this analysis was not new, and had echoes of much that had been said in earlier debates, this time a few leading individuals determined that the response should be both radical and permanent. The response was coordinated by the newly-established Council for Management Education and Development (now the National Forum for Management Education and Development (NFMED)) under the energetic and visionary leadership of Bob (now Sir Bob) Reid, formerly of Shell UK and the British Railways Board.

Under the umbrella of NFMED a series of employer-led working parties tackled the problem of defining what it was that managers should be able to do, and how this differed for people at different levels in their organizations; how this satisfactory ability to perform might be verified; and how an appropriate structure of management qualifications could be put in place. This work drew upon the methods used to specify vocational standards in industry and commerce, and led to the development and introduction of competence-based management standards and qualifications. In this context, competence is defined as the ability to perform the activities within an occupation or function to the standards expected in employment.

It is this competence-based approach that is new in our thinking about the manager's capabilities. It is also what is new about this series of books, in that they are designed to support both this new structure of management standards, and of development activities based on it. The series was originally commissioned to support the Institute of Management's Certificate and

Diploma qualifications, which were one of the first to be based on the new standards. However, these books are equally appropriate to any university, college or indeed company course leading to a certificate in management or diploma in management studies.

The standards were specified through an extensive process of consultation with a large number of managers in organizations of many different types and sizes. They are therefore employment based and employer supported. And they fill the gap that Mangham and Silver identified – now we do have a language to describe what it is employers want their managers to be able to do – at least in part.

If you are engaged in any form of management development leading to a certificate or diploma qualification conforming to the national management standards, then you are probably already familiar with most of the key ideas on which the standards are based. To achieve their key purpose, which is defined as achieving the organization's objectives and continuously improving its perform-ance, managers need to perform four key roles: managing operations, managing finance, managing people and managing information. Each of these key roles has a sub-structure of units and elements, each with associated performance and assessment criteria.

The reason for the qualification 'in part' is that organizations are different, and jobs within them are different. Thus the generic management standards probably do not cover all the management competencies that you may need to possess in your job. There are almost certainly additional things, specific to your own situation in your own organization, that you need to be able to do. The standards are necessary, but almost certainly not sufficient. Only you, in discussion with your boss, will be able to decide what other capabilities you need to possess. But the standards are a place to start, a basis on which to build. Once you have demonstrated your proficiency against the standards, it will stand you in good stead as you progress through your organization, or change jobs.

So how do the new standards change the process by which you develop yourself as a manager? They change the process of development, or of gaining a management qualification, quite a lot. It is no longer a question of acquiring information and facts, perhaps by being 'taught' in some classroom environ-ment, and then being tested to see what you can recall. It involves demonstrating, in a quite specific way, that you can do certain things to a particular standard of performance. And because of this, it puts a much greater onus on you to manage your own development, to decide how you can demonstrate any particular competence, what evidence you need to present, and how you can collect it. Of course, there will always be people to advise and guide you in this, if you need help.

But there is another dimension, and it is to this that this series of books is addressed. While the standards stress ability to perform, they do not ignore the traditional knowledge base that has been associated with management studies. Rather, they set this in a different context. The standards are supported by 'underpinning knowledge and understanding' which has three components:

- Purpose and context, which is knowledge and understanding of the manager's objectives, and of the relevant organizational and environmental influences, opportunities and values.
- Principles and methods, which is knowledge and understanding of the theories, models, principles, methods and techniques that provide the basis of competent managerial performance.
- Data, which is knowledge and understanding of specific facts likely to be important to meeting the standards.

Possession of the relevant knowledge and understanding underpinning the standards is needed to support competent managerial performance as specified in the standards. It also has an important role in supporting the transferability of management capabilities. It helps to ensure that you have done more than learned 'the way we do things around here' in your own organization. It indicates a recognition of the wider things which underpin competence, and that you will be able to change jobs or organizations and still be able to perform effectively.

These books cover the knowledge and understanding underpinning the management standards, most specifically in the category of principles and methods. But their coverage is not limited to the minimum required by the standards, and extends in both depth and breadth in many areas. The authors have tried to approach these underlying principles and methods in a practical way. They use many short cases and examples which we hope will demonstrate how, in practice, the principles and methods, and knowledge of purpose and context plus data, support the ability to perform as required by the management standards. In particular we hope that this type of presentation will enable you to identify and learn from similar examples in your own managerial work.

You will already have noticed that one consequence of this new focus on the standards is that the traditional 'functional' packages of knowledge and theory do not appear. The standard textbook titles such as 'quantitative methods', 'production management', 'organizational behaviour' etc. disappear. Instead, principles and methods have been collected together in clusters that more closely match the key roles within the standards. You will also find a small degree of overlap in some of the volumes, because some principles and methods support several of the individual units within the standards. We hope you will find this useful reinforcement.

Having described the positive aspects of standards-based management development, it would be wrong to finish without a few cautionary remarks. The developments described above may seem simple, logical and uncontroversial. It did not always seem that way in the years of work which led up to the introduction of the standards. To revert to the revolution analogy, the process has been marked by ideological conflict and battles over sovereignty and territory. It has sometimes been unclear which side various parties are on – and indeed how many sides there are! The revolution, if well advanced, is not at an end. Guerrilla warfare continues in parts of the territory.

Perhaps the best way of describing this is to say that, while competence-based standards are widely recognized as at least a major part of the answer to improving managerial performance, they are not the whole answer. There is still some debate about the way competencies are defined, and whether those in the standards are the most appropriate on which to base assessment of managerial performance. There are other models of management competencies than those in the standards.

There is also a danger in separating management performance into a set of discrete components. The whole is, and needs to be, more than the sum of the parts. Just like bowling an off-break in cricket, practising a golf swing or forehand drive in tennis, you have to combine all the separate movements into a smooth, flowing action. How you combine the competencies, and build on them, will mark your own individual style as a manager.

We should also be careful not to see the standards as set in stone. They determine what today's managers need to be able to do. As the arena in which managers operate changes, then so will the standards. The lesson for all of us as managers is that we need to go on learning and developing, acquiring new skills or refining existing ones. Obtaining your certificate or diploma is like passing a mile post, not crossing the finishing line.

All the changes and developments of recent years have brought management qualifications, and the processes by which they are gained, much closer to your job as a manager. We hope these books support this process by providing bridges between your own experience and the underlying principles and methods which will help you to demonstrate your competence. Already, there is a lot of evidence that managers enjoy the challenge of demonstrating competence, and find immediate benefits in their jobs from the programmes based on these new-style qualifications. We hope you do too. Good luck in your career development.

Paul Jervis

Introduction

Sir Alastair Grant, Chairman and Chief Executive, Argyll Group plc, shows how leadership and a striving for excellence can penetrate every corner of an organization:

'I have a dream about the future of Safeway. One day we shall have five hundred stores, each perfectly adapted to the needs of the community it serves; we shall sell twenty thousand products of which a third will be Safeway own brand; these own brands will match or beat the quality of the leading proprietary brands; we shall trade seven days a week and every minute that we are open, we shall fully satisfy every customer.

We shall be known and loved by every consumer; known and respected by every supplier; known and admired by every financial institution; known and valued by every member of government; known and understood by every journalist.

We are, I judge, about sixty percent of the way towards my dream. Our marketing reflects both where we are and where we want to be. I apply a marketing point of view to pretty well everything we do and I work at making the idea of marketing pervasive throughout the business.'

Meeting customer needs is a key objective for every manager. It can ensure that every day-to-day decision, every communication, every business process is focused on customers' real needs. While many companies limit their customer service initiatives to direct customer-facing activities, this book shows that there are a wide variety of actions that can be utilized to improve relations with customers – from making it easier for customers to place orders to developing customized products and services designed specifically for a customer.

Beginning with the importance of customer service and customer focus standards, this book contains advice, guidance and tips that can be put into action by managers with varying levels of resource. Together, these activities can help an organization develop a practical customer focus with the following characteristics:

1   The right degree of management commitment to customer service
2   A high level of staff understanding and awareness of customer service
3   A 'customer-focused' organization
4   The existence of measurable customer service standards
5   The existence of suitable customer feedback mechanisms
6   The existence of suitable complaints management procedures
7   A high level of customer retention
8   Customer-focused product development processes
9   Commitment to quality service delivery

The activities can be used as the basis of a structured, comprehensive customer service programme, or used selectively to improve performance in specific aspects of customer service, such as:

■   Building a team
■   Focusing on the customer
■   Customer service standards
■   Customer contact
■   Handling complaints
■   Customer relationships
■   The service contribution
■   Adding value
■   Making it easy to buy
■   Freeing people for customer service
■   Measuring customer service performance

This book provides all the information managers need to put the programmes into action. The activities can be used to improve performance in different aspects of customer service, or they can provide a framework for companies who are new to customer service – helping them to get a broad view of customer service and establish priorities.

1 Are you customer- focused?

Before we can meet customer needs, we have to understand who our customers are and what influences them when they are buying. However, many people within an organization feel that they do not have customers. In this chapter, therefore, we concentrate on the concept of 'internal customers'. You will gain an understanding of why you are asked to carry out some of your operations in a specific way to meet the needs of external customers. When everyone in an organization understands their role in meeting customer needs, the organization can be described as customer-focused.

WHAT IS A CUSTOMER?

A customer is an individual or group of individuals to whom you provide one or more products or services. You may receive goods or services in return or be paid through a third party who may also be your customer. These exchanges form a series of links in a chain which joins with other chains and drives not only organizations but also industries and economies.

In purely economic terms, each transaction must contain benefits to each party, i.e. a price which is acceptable to the customer and which provides you with sufficient rewards (or profits) to induce you to continue with the enterprise. In the non-profit or voluntary sectors, in other sectors such as public services and in internal markets, profit may not be definable in monetary terms. However, there must still be a satisfactory balance of benefits for both parties.

In your own job you will already have worked out most of your customers and will be thinking that you have some clear idea of their motivations. This exercise will help to clarify your role and responsibilities.

Write down the following column headings:

- My customers
- What I provide
- What I receive as a result
- Who I receive it from

Now write in the names of each of your customers, listing the other items against each customer. You should also consider who you may have missed out. When you feel that you have completed your list of customers, consider each column in turn, ask yourself the following questions and indicate your choices. In the 'My customers' column, identify:

- Which customer is most important to you
- Which is the most important customer as far as your boss is concerned
- Which is the most important customer to your company as a whole

In the 'What I provide' column, try to identify the provision which is most important to:

- You
- Your boss
- Your organization as a whole
- Your customers

In the columns headed 'What I receive as a result' and 'Who I receive it from', carry out a similar exercise. If you only have internal customers, you may not find it easy to carry out this exercise at first, but when you have put some effort into it, you will find that you know much more about your job and the workings of your department.

Complete this exercise by identifying a customer on your list who has direct contact with external customers. List the things which you do which enable that person or department to serve that external customer well. Can you identify improvements which you could make in your service which would result in an improved service to that external customer?

Here is how a major European telecommunications company views the importance of internal customer service.

> Quality and self-assessment are vital to any company's success, and involves every employee in the company. We all aim to identify best practice for our own jobs and try to beat it. The secret is continuous improvement – making lots of small changes work, rather than trying to force through one major change.
> In our experience, this approach is good for business. Improvements in our self-assessment scores are reflected in increased profit and customer satisfaction performance. The quality initiatives and continuous improvement programmes we have undertaken have helped us to maintain our leading position and we believe self-assessment and continuous improvement amongst all employees will continue to be an integral part of our business strategy.

WHY INTERNAL CUSTOMER SERVICE IS IMPORTANT

> 'You can't sell our department like soap powder. Customer service is fine for consumer products ... we don't need customer service here. We've been delivering a good service for years; the company needs us.'

Does this sound familiar? It's a protest that is repeated throughout every department in every sector of industry. 'We provide an essential activity to the company.' If you think that customer service is not important, ask yourself some questions:

- How will new technology affect the demand for your services?
- How easy is it to obtain funding for staff or new departmental systems?
- What would happen if your board decided to cut your departmental budget to reduce costs?
- Has your company considered outsourcing your department's activities?
- Are you attracting and retaining the right calibre of people?

Problems facing internal departments

- Many internal services are intangible. Internal customers do not always recognize the benefits or the value of a service.
- Services, unlike products, may not be essential to the success of a business. A factory could operate without functions like marketing, training or personnel, but it could not operate without raw materials, machinery or power.
- A factory manager could easily assess the benefits of an extra machine by measuring the increase in output, but could the benefit of additional investment in your department be measured so easily?
- How does a manager compare different departmental offers and what is the 'best buy'?

To succeed, you have to undertake a number of initiatives:

- Raise customer awareness of the quality and value of your departmental service
- Convince decision makers in your organization that your department makes an important contribution to corporate success
- Convince staff that your department's service is the best available.

INTERNAL 'CUSTOMERS' HAVE A CHOICE

An internal department has to bid for resources – companies do not fund a department without question. They compare the cost benefits with other investments and commit resources in line with corporate objectives. You therefore have to position your department as a valuable corporate resource that will prove to be a worthwhile investment. They also compare the cost benefits of an internal service with outsourcing. You have to demonstrate that your service can add real value to the organization.

TOWARDS AN INTERNAL CUSTOMER SERVICE STRATEGY

Do you know who your customers are? It may seem obvious, but many people in internal departments don't even realize they have customers. By listing people who might be your 'customers' and analysing the standard of service they

Table 1.1

Customer	Requirements
Staff	
Supervisors/departmental managers	
Senior executives	
Functional specialists	
Finance managers	
Information systems/data	
Processing staff	

should expect from you, you can develop a customer service policy. Table 1.1 can be used as a basis for planning and discussion with your team.

To help define the customer requirements on the right-hand side of the table, you should list the aspects of your service that are most important to different groups. These might include:

- Quality of service
- Speed of response to enquiries
- Timely delivery
- Attitude of staff
- Quality of management information
- Flexibility
- Ease of access for enquiries

When you have defined the aspects of service that are most important to different groups, you should write these down in the form of a 'service commitment' and tell your customers that you are now operating those standards.

MARKETING AN INTERNAL DEPARTMENT

A major insurance company found that departments within the organization did not understand the role of the marketing department. They carried out an internal marketing exercise to raise the profile of the department, build understanding and help people use its services more effectively. The example can be used as a template for marketing the services of other departments.

- How well do people within your organization understand the role of specific departments and the contribution they can make to the business?

- Are they aware of the full range of services available from the department or the skills of the departmental team?

The Marketing Communications team

We know that you are under pressure to deliver results with limited resources. We can help by taking responsibility for planning and running your marketing programmes. By speaking to us, you'll find that the Marketing Communications team has the skills and experience you'll need to find the right support solution.

We can work with you on overall promotional strategy or provide support for a specific tactical promotional task. Together, we can help you formulate the brief and identify the best creative partners for the task. We take the hassle away by managing the project and arranging distribution and, if you need funding, we have access to central funding for approved projects. We also monitor feedback to campaigns to see how useful they were, measure response levels and assess cost and value. That way we learn from every campaign.

Working with Marketing Communications

By combining your understanding of the marketplace with our expertise in marketing communications, we can add real value to our activities. We must all become champions of the brand and, together, we can develop support solutions that win business and strengthen customer loyalty.

We want to make it as easy as possible for you to work with the Marketing Communications team, and you can help us meet your goals by giving us plenty of advance warning so that we both work within realistic schedules, whenever possible. Timing is particularly important because the later a job is left, the more it is likely to cost.

We are always ready to meet and help you put your plans and initiatives into action. Please give us a call and we'll be delighted to have an introductory discussion.

UNDERSTANDING CUSTOMER NEEDS

Whether you are dealing with internal or external customers, it is important to look at service from the customer's point of view. What does the customer want? How does the customer feel about a product or service? To help you develop that empathy, you may find it useful to consider some of the problems you have faced as a consumer:

- What are your worst experiences when travelling?
- Have you had any holidays that went badly wrong?
- What about the car repair that dragged on or the story about the bank?

Now step back and look at the problem:

- Why were you upset?
- What were your expectations and why were they important?

You should then consider how the service could be improved and explain how this will enhance the customer's experience.

Customer service is everyone's responsibility. It is too easy to say 'It's not my problem' and pass the buck. While a department may not be individually or directly responsible for the problem or its solution, it may be able to contribute to the solution. Effective team work helps to improve overall standards of customer service, so it is important that everyone understands the problem their company faces and develops an attitude for sharing problems.

Sharing the problem

Which department has direct responsibility for solving the problem?
Which other departments have indirect responsibility for solving the problem?
How could the other departments contribute to the solution?
What skills would be required within the other departments?
Do staff attitudes need to be changed?

In the following examples, consider who is responsible and what can be done to improve the standard of service to the customer.

Wrong parts

A customer rents a new television and video from the local showroom. The engineer turns up at the customer's home to install the equipment, only to find that the wrong remote control has been supplied and the video has a fault. The engineer blames the warehouse for failing to check the consignment before delivery. The warehouse manager blames the quality manager for failing to meet requirements. The quality manager blames the supervisor for failing to check the staff's work. The local showroom manager blames the engineer for failing to check that he was fully prepared for the installation. Whose fault was it and what can be done to avoid a recurrence?

Nightmare holiday

After looking through a travel brochure, a customer books a package holiday through a travel agent. The hotel is not up to the customer's expectations – there is no sea view as promised in the brochure, the beach is certainly not 'a few minutes from the hotel', and the hotel swimming pool is not yet completed. The customer asks the travel agent for a refund. The travel agent blames the holiday company for failing to check the facilities. The holiday company blames the hotel for failing to provide the agreed facilities. Whose fault was it and what can be done to avoid a recurrence?

Service breakdown

The customer buys a used car from a local dealer. He books a service and takes a day's holiday so that he can deliver and collect the car. On the day, he is advised to collect the car at 5 o'clock. However, when he arrives to collect it, he is told that the car is not ready. A part was not available and the car cannot be driven. The customer now has no means of transport for getting to an important business meeting the next day. The service receptionist blames the parts department for not having the right parts stock. The parts manager blames the service department for not advising him of likely service requirements. The dealer manager blames the service manager for not advising the customer of the problem. Whose fault was it and what can be done to avoid a recurrence?

HOW DIFFERENT DEPARTMENTS CONTRIBUTE TO CUSTOMER SERVICE

Customer service is everyone's responsibility – or is it? In practice, it is often left to staff in sales, marketing or customer service – the people who are in regular contact with customers and who are in the best position to influence them.

The reality is that the actions and attitudes of everyone in an organization have a direct or indirect impact on the customer. By taking appropriate management actions, it is possible to improve the customer service performance of each individual, group or department. However, to make the best use of resources, it is essential to identify the most important customer service contributors and to impose priorities on improvement programmes.

Listed below are thirteen departments found in a typical manufacturing company. Consider the contribution of each department to customer service and number the departments in order of priority.

Sales
Manufacturing
Service
Marketing
Personnel
Customer service
Quality

Distribution
Purchasing
Design and development
Communications
Training
Administration

You could also assess each department's contribution and give it a score on a scale of 1–10. This can indicate comparative performance and highlight areas for improvement.

COMPETENCE SELF-ASSESSMENT

1 Describe the chain of people in your organization who represent your customers and suppliers when you carry out two of your main responsibilities.
2 Describe the chain of suppliers and customers in a manufacturing business such as cars.
3 Describe the chain of suppliers and customers in a service business such as air travel.
4 Prepare a profile of an internal department which represents one of your most important customers.
5 What are the most important factors affecting you as a customer if you are buying a car, a stereo system, a jar of coffee, or a personal gift for your partner?
6 Describe how could you improve your service to an internal department. How would this benefit your own department?
7 Write a memo to a head of department with whom you deal regularly, outlining how you intend to improve your service to that department.
8 Which departments in your organization make the most important contribution to quality customer service?
9 Describe how you would increase understanding of your department's role in customer service.
10 Prepare a plan to improve your personal effectiveness within your department. Describe how that would benefit the department.

2 How do customers buy?

This chapter outlines the techniques used by marketing professionals to analyse customer needs and identify buying factors. You can apply these techniques to your own activities, even if you are not dealing with external customers. The chapter will help you to understand the important differences between consumers and business customers and to respond with products and services that meet customers' real needs.

CONSUMER AND BUSINESS MARKETS

Before analysing customers in detail, it is important to decide whether your main markets are consumer or business-to-business:

- Business-to-business products and services are bought by organizations for use in producing other goods and services. They may be materials and components which form part of another product, or services that enable a business to produce its final product more efficiently.
- Consumer products are bought by individuals and house-holds for their own use.

Although the two sectors are regarded as separate, a number of products can be found in both sectors. Companies that market their products to specific sectors may have opportunities to expand their business. Some examples illustrate the process.

Electricity

- Consumers want reliable service at a reasonable cost.
- Business users want cost effective energy source plus added value services such as energy consultancy and management.

Television

- Consumers want an attractive unit, providing entertainment.
- Business users want rugged equipment to provide business information.

Car

- Consumers want prestige affordable motoring.
- Business owners want cost-effective transport.

Accounting software

- Consumers want simple packages for home finance.
- Business users want powerful systems to control business.

Consumer and business marketing techniques

Traditionally, consumer and business-to-business marketing techniques have been separated. This is based on a simplistic distinction between purchasing patterns and marketing techniques. Many textbooks describe the differences between consumer and business-to-business markets in the following way:

- Consumers buy for their own consumption while business buyers purchase on behalf of an organization.
- Consumer purchasing decisions are made by individuals, while business decisions are taken by teams.
- Consumer buying decisions are emotional, while business decisions are wholly rational.
- Consumer marketing tends to be dominated by mass market, short-term promotional techniques such as advertising and sales promotion, while business marketing uses targeted marketing techniques such as direct mail, exhibitions or press relations.

However, these distinctions are no longer clearcut, as consumer products manufacturers are beginning to utilize direct marketing, business marketeers utilize sales promotion techniques and research indicates that personal opinion and emotions play an equally important part in business buying decisions.

UNDERSTANDING CONSUMER PURCHASING

Every consumer is influenced by factors which change and vary in importance throughout their lives. These are the most important factors to consider when you try to understand the buying motives of consumers:

- Gender
- Age
- Marital status
- Children in household
- Income
- Socio-economic groups
- Occupation
- Personal financial management
- Home ownership
- Location
- Life cycle/sagacity
- Geodemographic systems
- Culture
- Lifestyle/psychographics
- Psychology

Gender

Certain consumer products and services appear to be aimed at specific sexes, for example clothes or specialist healthcare products. However, in reality, there are very few products or services which are not bought by both sexes.

Age

A consumer's age may provide some clues to their lifestyle and their interests. Products may be specifically targeted at an age group, for example retirement homes, Club 18–30 holidays, or the Puffin Book Club for children. Age groups are often grouped in decades starting at 15: 15–18, 18–20, 21–25, 25–34, 35–44, 45–54, 55–64, 65+.

Marital status

Marital status is a significant factor when it is combined with other factors such as children and income. Certain products or services may be aimed at people of a specific marital status, for example food and household products aimed at married couples, or small cars aimed at prosperous young single people. The categories are: single, married, divorced/separated, widowed.

Children in household

The presence of children in a household can have a significant effect on the disposable income of the household, its lifestyle, attitudes and consumption patterns. There is a vast difference in disposable income between single-income families with children and two-income families without children. The age of the children also affects disposable income.

Income

Income is described in two ways – net or gross. Net income is after tax and any other basic living costs have been deducted, whereas gross income is total income before tax and deductions. Not everyone is prepared to provide truthful answers about their income, so income is normally stated in £5000 or £10 000 bands. Lower income bands are often broken into smaller amounts to reflect the greater importance of an increase. The bands are: up to £5000, £5000–7500, £7500–10 000,   £10 000–12 500,   £12 500–15 000,   £15 000–25 000, £25 000–35 000, £35 000–45 000, £45 000–55 000, £55 000–65 000, over £65 000.

Socio-economic groups

The socio-economic groups most commonly used in the UK were developed as a rationalization of social class in the 1950s. However, they are severely flawed both in their structure and in their value as a model of today's society. In 1981, the Market Research Society published an evaluation of social grades which covers five socio-economic or social class groupings: A, B, C1, C2, D and E.

A   Higher managerial, administrative or professional
B   Intermediate managerial, administrative or professional
C1 Supervisory, clerical, junior administrative or professional
C2 Skilled manual workers
D   Semi-skilled and unskilled manual workers
E   State pensioners, widows, casual and lowest grade earners.

Occupation

Occupation is often too complex to help us discern its value as a factor in buying behaviour. In fact, there are few pieces of research where the actual occupation is recorded, apart from the National Readership Survey. Most occupation research tends to use the same categories as socio-economic groupings. However, the research may also include information on the sector in which the respondent is employed, for example teaching, civil service, engineering or the professions.

Personal financial management

A consumer's use of credit and their approach to money can be useful factors in evaluating buying behaviour. Ownership of credit cards, and the number and type of bank and building society accounts are not just indicators of financial well-being, they may also have a bearing on the willingness or the ability of the consumer to purchase certain types of product or service.

Home ownership

Home ownership results in certain needs and responsibilities which correlate directly with purchasing patterns. There has been a major shift in home ownership in recent years and, despite the recession, many more people own their home today, compared with the beginning of the 1980s.

Location

Where a consumer lives may have an important bearing on buying behaviour. Certain products or services may be limited to specific locations, and there are cultural and economic factors which predominate in certain regions. Rural and urban consumers differ, and there are also significant differences between inner-city, council estate and suburban consumers.

COMBINATIONS OF FACTORS

We can increase our understanding of buyer behaviour when we combine several factors together, for example the effect of children on family disposable income. Combining income with home ownership, location, partner's status and number and ages of children can help to identify the propensity and ability to buy certain products or services. By using different types of information in combination, we can create more sophisticated descriptions of consumers and their buying potential.

Life cycle/sagacity

Many of the buying factors come together to create an environment where certain types of behaviour may predominate. Using basic demographic data, for example, it is possible to put together a general model of the different stages of a person's life. One such model was created by William D. Wells and George Gubar[1] in America during the 1960s. They identified nine stages in what they called the family life cycle:

1 Bachelor stage: young, single people not living at home
2 Newly married couples: young, no children
3 Full nest I: youngest child under six
4 Full nest II: youngest child six or over
5 Full nest III: older married couples with dependent children
6 Empty nest I: older married couples, no children at home
7 Empty nest II: older married couples, retired, no children at home
8 Solitary survivor: in labour force
9 Solitary survivor: retired.

Although the concept is a good one, it does not address the true variety of modern society. It assumes a 'normal family life' and ignores the variety of normal family lifestyles which includes single-parent families, divorced or unmarried single people living on their own, mature single people living with or caring for elderly relatives.

The other drawback to such systems is their applicability. 'Sagacity', developed by the research company RSL Ltd, uses the huge data sets available from the National Readership Survey to provide a definition and classification of individuals (see Figure 2.1).

Geodemographic systems

The geodemographic classification system classifies groups of people according to where they live, and according to a wide range of demographic, socio-economic and housing data which are available on small areas. The ACORN system (A Classification of Residential Neighbourhoods) was created by identifying different variables which could be obtained from the census at enumeration district level – small areas which contain approximately 150 households. The data give us, for example, the percentage of the population of each enumeration district in each of the different age bands, the percentage of men and women to be found in each of the enumeration districts and the percentage of homes with different types of facilities. The process which can be seen in Figure 2.2 provides a meaningful range of neighbourhood types. Systems like this tend to be effective discriminators of purchasing behaviour, allowing marketers to gain a greater understanding of the groups of people who buy specific products or services. It has been possible to refine the classifications further and allocate the area types to area codes as small as postal codes which contain approximately fifteen to twenty homes.

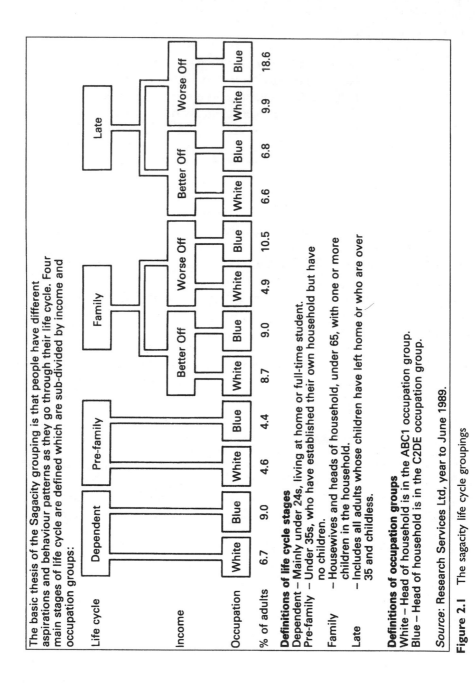

The basic thesis of the Sagacity grouping is that people have different aspirations and behaviour patterns as they go through their life cycle. Four main stages of life cycle are defined which are sub-divided by income and occupation groups:

Life cycle	Dependent		Pre-family		Family					Late			
Income					Better Off		Worse Off			Better Off		Worse Off	
Occupation	White	Blue	White	Blue	White	Blue	White	Blue	White	Blue	White	Blue
% of adults	6.7	9.0	4.6	4.4	8.7	9.0	4.9	10.5	6.6	6.8	9.9	18.6

Definitions of life cycle stages
Dependent – Mainly under 24s, living at home or full-time student.
Pre-family – Under 35s, who have established their own household but have
no children.
Family   – Housewives and heads of household, under 65, with one or more
children in the household.
Late   – Includes all adults whose children have left home or who are over
35 and childless.

Definitions of occupation groups
White – Head of household is in the ABC1 occupation group.
Blue – Head of household is in the C2DE occupation group.

Source: Research Services Ltd, year to June 1989.

Figure 2.1   The sagacity life cycle groupings

ACORN stands for 'A Classification Of Residential Neighbourhoods'. The system was developed by CACI. The table below shows ACORN's 38 neighbourhood types, the 11 groups they form, and their share of the GB population of 54 086 798 in 1987. ACORN is based on the Government's Census of Great Britain conducted in 1981. The 1987 populations of the 1981 census neighbourhoods are derived from CACI's proprietary demographic model of Great Britain.

ACORN types		% of 1987 population		ACORN groups	
A 1	Agricultural villages	2.6	3.5	Agricultural areas	A
A 2	Areas of farms and smallholdings	0.8			
B 3	Post-war functional private housing	4.3			
B 4	Modern private housing, young families	3.5		Modern family	
B 5	Established private family housing	5.9	17.1	housing, higher	B
B 6	New detached houses, young families	2.8		incomes	
B 7	Military bases	0.6			
C 8	Mixed owner-occupied and council estates	3.5		Older housing of	
C 9	Small town centres and flats above shops	4.1	17.8	intermediate	C
C10	Villages with non-farm employment	4.8		status	
C11	Older private housing, skilled workers	5.5			
D12	Unmodernized terraces, older people	2.5		Older terraced	
D13	Older terraces, lower income families	1.4	4.3	housing	D
D14	Tenement flats lacking amenities	0.4			
E15	Council estates, well-off older workers	3.5			
E16	Recent council estates	2.8	13.0	Council estates –	E
E17	Better council estates, younger workers	4.9		category I	
E18	Small council houses, often Scottish	1.9			
F19	Low rise estates in industrial towns	4.6			
F20	Inter-war council estates, older people	2.9	9.0	Council estates –	F
F21	Council housing, elderly people	1.4		category II	
G22	New council estates in inner cities	2.0			
G23	Overspill estates, higher unemployment	3.0	7.2	Council estates –	G
G24	Council estates with some overcrowding	1.5		category III	
G25	Council estates with greatest hardship	0.6			
H26	Multi-occupied older housing	0.4		Mixed inner	
H27	Cosmopolitan owner-occupied terraces	1.1	3.8	metropolitan	H
H28	Multi-let housing in cosmopolitan areas	0.7		areas	
H29	Better-off cosmopolitan areas	1.7			
I 30	High status non-family areas	2.1		High status non-	
I 31	Multi-let big old houses and flats	1.5	4.2	family areas	I
I 32	Furnished flats, mostly single people	0.5			
J 33	Inter-war semis, white collar workers	5.7		Affluent	
J 34	Spacious inter-war semis, big gardens	5.0	15.9	suburban	J
J 35	Villages with wealthy older communities	2.9		housing	
J 36	Detached houses, exclusive suburbs	2.3			
K37	Private houses, well-off older residents	2.3	3.8	Better-off	K
K38	Private flats, older single people	1.6		retirement areas	
U39	Unclassified	0.5	0.5	Unclassified	U
		100.0			

Figure 2.2 ACORN profile of Great Britain. *Source*: CACI Market Analysis, 1989, © CACI

Culture

Cultural influences can affect buying behaviour in a number of ways. In the UK, we have a number of regional and racial cultural variations which influence purchase decisions. These influences can be very subtle, and many studies have been carried out to try to understand the role of culture. Within each cultural group there are smaller groups each with their own distinctive values. Qualitative research, which is discussed later, is used extensively by marketers who wish to understand cultural issues.

Lifestyle/psychographics

As Philip Kotler[2] points out, 'Lifestyle attempts to profile a person's way of being and acting in the world'. There are two main approaches to lifestyle classification. One uses a long questionnaire broken down into four main topics:

1   Activities such as hobbies, clubs and entertainment
2   Interests such as home, food and fashion
3   Opinions on such topics as politics, education and economics
4   Basic demographic information on each respondent.

The responses are analysed to identify clusters of people with similar lifestyles. When combined with demographic data and analysed against purchasing data, these lifestyle groups can provide valuable insight into consumer motivations. The research company BMRB has carried out a great deal of work in this area using lifestyle questionnaires which have been attached to their large consumer survey, Target Group Index.

The second type of lifestyle classification, developed in the USA by Arnold Mitchell[3] of SRI International, is based on the same technique, but approaches the classification from a psychological point of view. Mitchell explored the values of the individuals in each group and identified nine development stages that people appeared to go through. Each stage affected the person's attitudes, behaviour and psychological needs:

- Need-driven stage
  – survivors or sustainers
- Inner- or outer-directed stage
  – I-am-me, experientials and societally conscious (inner)
  – belongers, emulators and achievers stages (outer)
- Integrated stage (achieved by only a small percentage)

In the UK, the market research company Taylor Nelson has developed and successfully used a similar classification system. Systems like this are interesting, but require a massive amount of research work. Their importance lies in their recognition of the value of each individual's personal interests and motivations.

Psychology

Adam Maslow[4] identified a hierarchy of needs (see Figure 2.3) which suggests that needs are felt at different levels by everyone:

- Basic physiological need for survival
- Need for protection and security
- Social needs such as love, belonging
- Esteem needs such as status or self-esteem
- Self-actualization needs which involve self-development.

UNDERSTANDING BUSINESS PURCHASING

This section looks at the business purchasing process in more detail – who makes the decisions, what they contribute to the decision-making process and what they need to know about your organization to select you as the preferred supplier.

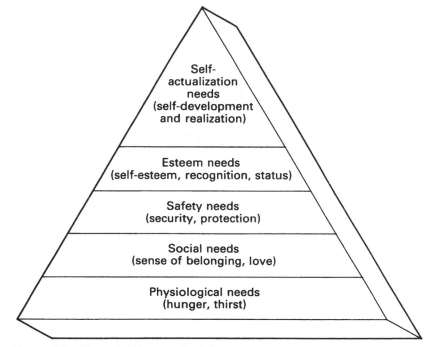

Figure 2.3 Maslow's hierarchy of needs

Although the influence of multiple decision makers has long been recognized in business-to-business purchasing, it is essential that you take positive steps to identify the role and contribution of each member. It is essential to know:

- Who drives the purchasing decisions?
- Who is in favour of your company?
- Who are your competitors close to?
- How are you and your competitors viewed by different members of the purchasing team?

By understanding the decision-making process, your organization can concentrate its resources on the most important customer service tasks. Constant research is essential to ensure:

- Your team are focusing on the right people at the right time. Purchasing situations are fluid and it would be easy to concentrate on the wrong members.
- The importance of team purchasing to the customers. The higher the value of the product to the customer, the more weight they will add to their purchasing teams.

In the automotive industry, for example, manufacturers are aligning their purchasing teams by component group so that they can improve their own purchasing professionalism and their negotiating power. Although sales of your product may be vital to the future of your company, that product may be of less significance to your customers.

INFLUENCING ALL DECISION MAKERS

The growth in team purchasing means that you must influence all team members and help them to make decisions in your favour. The situation is complicated by the fact that the influence of team members varies during the purchasing cycle:

- Purchasing staff and departmental managers may have considerable influence in the early stages when a specification is being drawn up.
- When proposals are being evaluated, technical staff may be more influential.
- Some members of the team may require more help in making a decision than others.

Research must be carefully focused to establish the relative status of different members. The next part of this section looks at the potential contribution of a number of different team members. This type of information is important if you are dealing with internal customers. You need to understand their concerns and requirements to deliver an effective service.

Example
When Just-In-Time (JIT) manufacturing first grew in importance, computer manufacturers who wanted to sell manufacturers systems to operate their JIT programmes had to help manufacturing teams understand not only the relationship between JIT and computers but also the management implications of introducing JIT before they could discuss the benefits of their computers over competitors. The manufacturing management teams did not understand how to make purchasing decisions in this area and the successful computer manufacturers were those who gave their customers a great deal of support.

Senior executives

Senior executives need an overview of the overall business benefits of a product or service and they seek reassurance that your organization is a capable supplier. Many companies try to move discussion of their products and services to board level to demonstrate that they are a strategic supplier.

Example
A manufacturer of advanced composite materials wanted to position the product as a means of improving competitive performance. Manufacturers who adopted composites instead of traditional materials would be able to offer their customers better performance, greater reliability, and a range of other benefits which would improve their competitive position. It was vital that senior executives realized the strategic importance because other members of the purchasing team might have rejected the product on the basis that it was more expensive than conventional materials and was more difficult to manufacture. The senior executive's strategic considerations might prevail over the team members concerned with immediate issues.

A senior executive will also be concerned with the long-term stability of the supplier. Any risk could be detrimental to the customer's own business and a senior executive needs to be convinced that your organization has the capability and the capacity to continue meeting long-term needs. Key information would include:

- Your track record and position in the market
- The size of your operations and your recent investment programmes
- Your record on quality
- The skills of your staff and details of any training programmes that you are using to improve performance
- Details of your recent financial performance and information on your management team
- Background information on your relations with other members of a group or holding company
- Your company's long-term direction and your plans for product or service development

Purchasing professionals

Purchasing professionals remain the key figures in a purchasing team. While they may not take sole responsibility for decision making, they are liable to be the team leaders and will remain your main point of contact. Many companies operate a preferred supplier programme and, to be recognized, you may have to meet a detailed list of criteria. The purchasing department would be instrumental in managing the list of approved suppliers even though the criteria were drawn up by other members of the team. Many of the preferred supplier programmes include vendor rating schemes which allow a customer to measure suppliers' continuing performance against a set of factors. These are part of a process of developing effective relationships with suppliers so that purchasing professionals can provide an even better service to their 'internal customers'.

Example
Japanese companies are perhaps best known for this positive attitude to supplier/customer relationships. An electrical component manufacturer described how teams of manufacturing and quality specialists from a customer company spent a week in his production department and made a list of suggestions that helped the supplier improve his own processes. The long-term result was that the customer enjoyed a better standard of service. While this

quality of relationship may be comparatively rare, it is important to develop effective relationships which help to improve the purchasing professional's status within his own organization.

What purchasing professionals look for

- Process improvements which make it easier to do business. For example, by introducing on-line ordering or single-line summary invoices, you can help to reduce the burden of paperwork which prevents purchasing departments from operating efficiently.
- Up-to-date information on status of orders can help them to manage their own operations more efficiently and product guides which are updated regularly will ensure that they provide their customers with the right quality of service.

Finance executives

Finance executives have ultimate control over purchasing budgets. The following are some of their key concerns:

- They seek reassurance that they are getting value for money and that their purchase represents the best return on investment.
- Large, complex purchases which involves major capital expenditure are likely to involve the finance executive.
- They consider alternative methods of financing the purchase and you may be able to improve your competitive position by offering flexible financial schemes such as leasing or deferred payments.
- They need to know how services such as training, contract maintenance or project management can save them money on through-life costs.
- They are interested in proposals which reduce supply chain costs. For example, manufacturing systems that reduce production costs, logistics services that cut the cost of distribution, performance improvements that reduce the cost of maintaining products, or outsourced services that reduce overheads can make a vital contribution to a customer's financial performance.

Technical staff

Technical staff are now a vital element in the purchasing team. They are responsible for improving the performance of the company products so that they can develop a competitive edge. You therefore need to be closely involved with the technical team at a number of different stages:

- When they are developing new products, you should be involved at the planning stages so that you can influence the design.
- When they are enhancing existing products you should be developing proposals to improve product performance.
- When they are moving into new markets you can support their activities by handling contract development services or by training their staff and enhancing their skills.
- You can provide them with a range of specialist technical services that enable them to provide a better service to their internal customers.

What technical staff need from you

- Provide information on your product performance – what it will do for their products. By providing high levels of technical information in an easily accessible form, you can help your customer's team design in your products.
- Offer application guides. Increasingly, these are available on computer software so that designers can integrate application data with their own product data.
- Consider joint development projects where suppliers undertake specialist design work not only improves working relationships, it also helps to ensure that your company is the preferred supplier on complex projects.
- Provide support if you are introducing new technology. You may need to help the technical decision makers understand and use new technology. Designers may be cautious if they have not used a material or component before.
- Provide them with test data and reports or run workshops and seminars to demonstrate the potential of the new product.
- Reassure specifiers that they are selecting products or services that will help them to improve their market performance. Your product should help them achieve better performance, greater reliability, lower operating costs, simpler handling, reduced maintenance or better value for money – factors that help them achieve market leadership.

Manufacturing managers

If you are introducing an innovative product or you have identified an opportunity to improve your customers' manufacturing operations or reduce costs, you need to influence manufacturing specialists. Focus on the manufacturing manager when the following conditions apply:

- You have identified opportunities to reduce manufacturing costs.
- Your product will require modifications to the customer's manufacturing process.
- Your customer is encountering production problems which affect his own competitive performance.

Example
An engineering component manufacturer who utilized value engineering needed to demonstrate how their products would reduce overall manufacturing costs. The company, which specialized in rolling bearings, had modified standard transmission bearings for specific applications. By customizing the housing and improving the integral sealing, the company was able to offer one-piece integrated components with a long life. The customer could use this integrated component to reduce the number of machining operations, simplify assembly and cut stock-holding costs. This reduced manufacturing costs and, combined with the savings in maintenance, contributed to lower through-life costs. To the rest of the purchasing team, the new integrated component appeared more expensive and represented a radical change in manufacturing and assembly processes, therefore it was important to ensure that the manufacturing manager understood the contribution of the component.

Service providers

If you provide professional services rather than products, you need to ensure that you are dealing with a service provider. Service providers are responsible for the following areas:

- Maintenance
- Training

- Administration
- Logistics
- Computer services and the other services that enable other business processes to operate efficiently

What service providers are looking for

- Ways of supplementing their own resources
- Opportunities to reduce the cost of their own operations by outsourcing services that are not used regularly or which require expensive scarce skills

Marketing staff

In a balanced project team, marketing specialists will provide important input, ensuring that the product or service adds value and helps the company develop a stronger competitive position. Marketing staff will play an important part in the decision-making process if the following conditions apply: your customers are seeking to improve their market position or your customers are entering new markets where you have a specific expertise.

What marketing departments are looking for

- Innovations which improve product performance
- Ways of reducing costs or increase reliability
- Opportunities to gain a stronger presence in the market

Departmental managers

Departmental managers are often the users of your products or services. They need to be reassured that they will benefit from dealing with a specific supplier and they play an important role in specifying the product and evaluating the performance of existing suppliers. The departmental manager will play an important part in the decision making if the following conditions apply:

- Your product or service has an impact on day-to-day operations.
- The department has experienced operating difficulties with your product or competitive products.
- The department is facing pressures which can be solved by your product or service.

The introduction of a new office system, for example, may result in improved departmental efficiency, better working conditions or total chaos! The departmental manager is under pressure from his or her own management team to meet corporate objectives and deliver higher standards of service, while reducing costs and making the best use of available resources. You need to be aware of these pressures so that you can tailor your product or service offering.

What departmental managers are looking for

■ Support. You need to work closely with the user department so that you can implement a new product or service that suits their working requirements and represents minimal disruption to their day-to-day activities.

■ Product suitability. You should also consult departmental managers to see how easily products or services meet their requirements.

RESEARCHING DECISION MAKERS

Although it is relatively simple to list the potential decision makers it is more difficult to identify who is actually involved in the process. Many decision makers may not have a direct role in a project team or they may be involved in only part of the purchasing process. Research is therefore more difficult and you need to look carefully at your research processes. The sales team in regular contact with the customer should be in the best position to identify the key decision makers but they may have limited contact within the organization and they may be overlooking key people. There are a number of other techniques for identifying the other influencers:

■ Formal independent research which asks companies how they buy different types of product or service. The survey may be limited to a specific group of customers or prospects or it can be carried out across a whole industry.

■ Published industry surveys on buying patterns. These provide broad guidelines to the key decision makers but need to be qualified by specific account research.

■ Joint projects where members of the customer team work with members of your team on a specific project. The relationships and the approval procedures that emerge provide useful clues to the hidden decision makers.

Research like this should be carried out continuously because purchase is a dynamic process. Members of the decision-making team may change their jobs and, as the purchasing process progresses through different stages, team members' individual contribution changes.

COMPETENCE SELF-ASSESSMENT

1 Prepare a profile of an individual customer who represents one of your most important customers.
2 What are the most important factors affecting you as a business customer if you are buying office equipment, company cars or contract catering?
3 Describe the members of a purchasing team for business travel, departmental computers, office stationery.
4 Give five examples of products or services which appeal to both consumer and business markets.
5 Select three current television commercials for consumer products and describe the type of consumer at whom the commercial is aimed.
6 Write a series of short letters describing the benefits of your department's services to the managing director, finance director, marketing director and a departmental manager.
7 If your organization provides products or services specifically for the consumer or business sector, describe how the product or service could be adapted for the sector you do not currently serve.
8 Describe your personal characteristics as a consumer.
9 Describe your actual or potential role in a company-wide purchasing team.
10 What factors are most important to you in selecting products or services for your department or organization?

REFERENCES

1 Ohmae, K. (1982) *The Mind of the Strategist*, Penguin, New York, p. 109.
2 Wells, W. D. and Gubar, G. (1966) Lifecycle concepts in marketing research, *Journal of Marketing Research*, November, p. 362.
3 Kotler, P. (1988), *The Principles of Marketing, Analysis, Planning, Implementation and Control* (6th edn), Prentice-Hall, New Jersey.
4 Mitchell, A. (1983) *The Nine American Life Styles*, Macmillan, New York.
5 Maslow, A. H. (1954) *Motivation and Personality*, Harper and Row, New York.
6 Howard J. A. and Sheth, J. N. (1969) *The Theory of Buyer Behaviour*, John Wiley, New York.
7 Engel, J., Kollat, D. and Blackwell, R. (1978) *Consumer Behaviour*, Dryden Press, New York
8 Sheth, J. N. (1974) *Models of Buyer Behaviour*, Harper and Row, New York.
9 Kotler, Philip *op. cit.*
10 Sheth, J. N. (1973) A model of industrial buyer behaviour, *Journal of Marketing Research*, October.
11 Webster, W. and Wind, Y. (1972) *Organizational Buyer Behaviour*, Prentice-Hall, New Jersey.

3 Researching customer requirements

We need to gather information before assessing how we might improve our service to customers. The process begins with research to gather data which can be used for making decisions, solving problems and monitoring your progress or that of your competitors. As well as formal research, there are many activities which can be used to find out more about customers. Technologies such as database management, document image processing and data warehousing enable organizations to distribute and exploit information more easily and get a clearer picture of customer requirements.

GETTING FAMILIAR WITH CUSTOMERS

How well do you know your customers' business, their markets, their plans, their competitors and their strengths and weaknesses? The more you know, the more easily you can identify their real needs and develop a service that wins and keeps business. Although you can find out a lot about your customers just by looking in your sales records, desk research is no substitute for getting out and meeting customers face to face. The sales team are doing that all the time, but it is unlikely that they will be responsible for delivering customer service. You need to meet the customers yourself. The following are some suggestions for increasing personal contact and improving customer relationships.

Arrange an informal customer visit

Many customers will appreciate the interest you are showing in their business – or invite customers to visit your premises. It provides a good chance for customer-facing staff to meet their opposite numbers and it can help to improve working relationships.

Attend exhibitions, seminars and conferences

You can find out what competitors are up to at the same time. Events like these are a good indicator of what customers believe is important to the success of their business.

Carry out customer care visits

Call on selected customers at intervals to discuss whether they are satisfied with the standard of service they are receiving from you. Ask if they have any specific concerns and ensure that you contact them again with an appropriate response.

Set up regular review meetings

This is a more formal process than the *ad hoc* customer care visits. Suppliers and customers agree to meet at regular intervals – annually, quarterly or monthly, depending on the complexity and importance of the business. There is likely to be a set agenda for reviewing performance in specific areas and there may be agreed standards that are used to measure performance.

Arrange briefing meetings for your customers

These meetings are not used to review progress or performance, but give you the opportunity to bring your customers up to date with new developments in your business or in your industry that might benefit them. For example, you might brief them on new technical developments or new legislation that is likely to impact on them. This type of meeting not only demonstrates your profession-alism, it also helps to add value to the customer relationship.

Hold a social

Many customers enjoy the chance to meet informally and talk shop. A social event could take place after a more formal meeting or it might be an event in its own right. Although the extravagant side of corporate hospitality has largely disappeared, social events remain an important part of business relationships.

Don't forget to take action

When you have made your visit, use the information you have gathered and make sure that you develop an action plan to improve standards of service in areas that customers feel are important.

WHAT SORT OF SERVICE DO CUSTOMERS WANT?

The point of research is not to gather data, but to find out what customers actually want from your department or your organization. Table 3.1 shows scores for the top ten customer issues from a survey of financial institution customers.

This survey gives a valuable insight into the type and quality of service customers want from an organization. Those are the issues that customers feel are important and those are the areas that the company must concentrate on if it is to strengthen its position even further. The survey also reveals how customers' perceptions of the importance of different factors are changing. Overall, the results confirm that the quality of relationships remain top of the agenda from the customer's point of view, while charges have fallen from top spot to third. In terms of customer service, that means:

■ Customers want companies to understand their business, so staff must find out all they can.

Table 3.1

Issue	Satisfaction (%)		
	A	B	C
Being supportive of my business	61	52	71
Understanding my business	62	75	59
Current account transaction charges	45	42	47
Speed of decisions (on lending)	67	45	82
Credibility and authority of main account contact	64	73	60
Continuity of main account contact	60	73	59
Autonomy of account contact in decisions that affect my business	58	73	62
Accessibility of main account contact	72	73	75
Speed of carrying out instructions	76	47	85
Reliable and efficient service in the branch	81	75	84

Table 3.2   How customers rate component suppliers

Factor	Company A	Satisfaction % Company B	Company C
Pre-sales advice	49	53	61
Quality of product	75	78	77
Technical support	83	74	85
Delivery	60	65	53
Innovative	85	64	89
Easy to deal with	65	63	75
New product development	88	62	85
Cooperation	63	55	80

■ Customers welcome regular, helpful contact, so the company must take every opportunity to keep in touch and provide support.

■ Customers want speedy, efficient service.

■ Customers prefer a long-term relationship with their main contact, so they should not be 'passed around'.

This research report lists factors that could affect relationships between a components manufacturer and key customers (Table 3.2).

CUSTOMER RESEARCH

This section explains how to use information on markets and customers to help you plan customer service programmes. Market research can be carried out within your own organization or by using the services of an external research agency.

Analysing customer information

Information is readily available in your own customer records that can help you to identify customer needs:

■ Who are your largest customers?

■ What percentage of your business do they represent?

■ How dependent are you on their business continuing at the same level or growing?

- Which of the large customers has the strongest growth prospects?
- Is there a risk that any of the customers might defect to competitors?
- How long have they been doing business with you?
- How strong is the relationship with key decision makers?
- How have levels of business changed over the past three years?
- Are there any significant developments which have affected these changes?
- What percentage of those customers' business do you handle?
- How could you increase your share?

Information from publications

What do your customers' corporate brochures or annual reports tell you about them?

- What are their major markets?
- What are their most important products?
- What new products have they introduced in the last year?
- What are their plans for growth?
- What problems have they identified in their marketplace?
- What are the success factors in their market?
- Who are their main competitors?

Information from other sources

You can get similar information from other sources. Ask your salesforce to provide a profile of your most important customers, using the questions in the section above. Maintain a file of press cuttings on your customers' activities using their trade publications as a source. Build a file of corporate and product literature on your customers' competitors and look for press information on their market.

Using the information

This information helps to build a profile of the direction your customers' business is taking. It would be used to shape future sales and marketing policy, but it also has a far more important role which may be overlooked – it should prompt you to ask 'How could our products and services help this customer overcome problems, realize opportunities or meet objectives?'

INFORMATION AND CUSTOMER SERVICE

Understanding your customers is the first step to developing positive, long-term relationships with them. The customer information you hold can be used in several important ways:

- To improve customer handling by making information available to staff responsible for sales, enquiries, helplines, order processing, complaints, service or other customer-facing activities
- To improve understanding of the customer's purchasing life cycle
- To identify opportunities to offer customers a range of other products or services tailored to their individual needs. Taken to its logical conclusion, this could enable you to deal with customers as individuals on a one-to-one basis – a very powerful form of niche marketing.

CUSTOMER RESEARCH TECHNIQUES

Telephone interviews

Telephone interviews are a quick and cost-effective way to obtain opinions from a sample of customers. A sample of customers are contacted by phone and asked a set series of questions.

Telephone interviews are quick. Large numbers of interviews can be conducted in a short space of time. Data can be gathered and processed quickly. They are also cost-effective; costs are considerably less than personal interviews. Telephone interviews are non-intrusive; a customer may be too busy for a personal interview, but is willing to spend time on the phone.

However, it can be difficult to reassure people that you are carrying out legitimate research and people may not be prepared to spend a long period of time on the telephone. It can also be difficult to get across complex concepts by telephone. This is an extract from a survey conducted by a local radio station to assess listening habits.

> Good evening, I'm carrying out a survey for a local radio station and I would be grateful if you could spare the time to answer a few questions.
> Do you ever listen to radio?
> How often do you listen – daily, weekly, occasionally?
> Do you listen at home, in the car at work?

What times of the day would you normally listen?
Which station or stations do you normally listen to?
Do you choose them for music, news, information or other reasons?
Can you receive any of the following stations in your area?

Postal surveys

Postal surveys are delivered directly to customers. Although they are a quick and relatively inexpensive method of obtaining information, it can be difficult to obtain a reasonable rate of response and the researcher has no control over the process. Postal surveys are inexpensive; costs include outward and return postage and stationery. They are precise and can be targeted at specific customers or prospects. They are voluntary and there is no pressure on the customer. However, response rates can be low and incentives may be needed to improve response rates. Responses can be incomplete and response times slow. Here is an example of a postal questionnaire.

Thank you for sparing a few minutes to fill in our customer service questionnaire. Your responses are of great value to us in identifying areas where we can improve our service to you. When you have completed the form please return it in the stamped addressed envelope provided.

1   While you were in the showroom did a member of staff acknowledge you?   YES/NO
2   Did the salesperson introduce themselves?   YES/NO
3   Which of the following questions did the salesperson ask?
    Style/range required   YES/NO
    Budget   YES/NO
    Accessories required   YES/NO
4   Did the salesperson provide any of the following?
    Brochure   YES/NO
    Details of the guarantee   YES/NO
    Price   YES/NO
    Business card   YES/NO

5   How satisfied were you with the sales/service you
received?
Very satisfied
Fairly satisfied
Not satisfied
If you would like to make any further comments please use
the space below.

Group discussions

A number of customers and prospects are invited to discuss a particular topic, usually under the guidance of a researcher. Discussions can be open ended; there is no limit placed on what the group can discuss. This can highlight important customer issues that the researcher may not be aware of. They can also be enjoyable; many customers welcome the opportunity to discuss products and services with their colleagues. Group discussions can be observed; one-way mirrors or closed circuit television can be used. They also provide customers with an opportunity to contribute to change.

However, they are not representative; they can be biased or influenced by a dominant member of the group and results cannot be easily quantified. The following is an example of a customer focus panel for a petrol retailers. The customers in this case are motorists and they include a cross-section of a petrol station's customer base:

- Business travellers
- Delivery drivers
- Long-distance lorry drivers
- Domestic drivers
- Elderly drivers
- Handicapped drivers

The aim was to find out what each of these motorists wanted from a petrol service station. The key issues were convenience of opening hours, ease of access, number of pumps, location, payment facilities, customer facilities such as toilets and drinks, and the availability of other products such as snacks, motoring products and, increasingly, the range of other products available in the forecourt. The information provided by the motorists' panel showed the retailer the direction in which he could expand his business and provided a valuable indication of the areas which needed improvement.

The second stage of the focus panel was to review the findings of the panel with the management team and to develop an action plan to make any improvements which had been identified. The information was also used as a basis for national planning. By putting together the information from panels around the country, the head office team were able to identify regional and national patterns in consumer requirements. This provided a valuable basis for planning national forecourt development programmes and providing the right level of regional and local support. The focus panels were held on a regional basis and this proved a valuable method of monitoring customers' response to the improvements that had been made at the suggestion of earlier focus panels. By showing that they were prepared to respond to motorists' concerns, the retailer was able to demonstrate high levels of customer care.

Personal interviews

In a personal interview a customer and an interviewer work through a series of predetermined questions such as a questionnaire. The interview can take place in a customer's home, office or in a public place. The interview can be pre-arranged by telephone, post or personal contact or they can be *ad hoc*.

Personal interviews allow in-depth discussion of complex topics. They provide greater control over response and ensure greater accuracy. The results are easy to analyse and meeting people in a working environment can give an indication of their real purchasing intents. However, the time and cost of recruiting interviewers and conducting interviews can be prohibitive and there is a risk of interviewer bias. The following is an example of a personal interview.

In order to plan communications with its largest client, a company carries out an audit of current perceptions by interviewing key decision makers. The audit is concerned with the relationship and image of the supplier from the customer's point of view. It compares the customer's views with those of the supplier and incorporates the customer's views of competitors. The audit compares the actual perceptions against current communications activities and highlights key communications actions needed to achieve the target perception. The audit was carried out by an independent research company who contacted decision makers by post and followed by telephone to arrange appointments. The following were the main questions they asked:

- How aware are you of the company?
- How aware are you of the following competitors?
- How would you rate the professionalism of sales contact?
- Does the sales team understand your business and your products?
- Does the company communicate its future strategies effectively?
- How would you rate the company and its competitors for product reliability?
- Do you believe the company makes an important contribution to the success of your organization?
- How do you rate the company's product line?

The audit identified the key areas for improving communications performance and it is essential that these messages should be communicated consistently in every form of contact with the customer.

ANALYSING COMPETITIVE ACTIVITY

By answering the following questions, you can build up a detailed picture of your competitors. You should then evaluate their performance in customer service.

How many competitors do you have?
Who are the most important competitors?
Are they direct or indirect competitors?
Where are your main competitors located?
How do they compare in size?
Who are your competitors' main customers?
Do competitors threaten any of your existing customers?
Which of your competitors' customers do you want to win?
Do they have the same product range as you?
How do their products compare?
How do prices compare?
What are their standards of customer service?
What do customers think of competitors?
Do you have any research which compares your company with competitors?
What are your main strengths compared with competitors?
What are your main weaknesses compared with competitors?

Listed below are fifteen factors that are important to quality service. On a scale of 1–10, how do you think your company and your three main competitors score on each of the factors. The results should be used as the basis for a programme of performance improvement.

Factor	You	Competitors
1 The degree of commitment to quality service		
2 The level of staff understanding and awareness of customer service		
3 How 'customer-focused' is the organization?		
4 The existence of measurable service standards		
5 The existence of suitable customer feed-back mechanisms		
6 The existence of suitable complaints management procedures		

7   The degree of customer retention
8   The customer focus of product develop-
    ment processes
9   Commitment to quality service delivery
10 Scope of pre-sales activity
11 Simplicity of enquiry and ordering
12 Quality of product/service delivery
13 Efficiency of purchase administration
14 Effectiveness of sales follow-up
15 Quality of after-sales support

USING BENCHMARKING TECHNIQUES

Benchmarking is a form of research that can be used to compare an organization's performance with other organizations who are regarded as demonstrating best practice. By comparing current performance with best practice, an organization can:

- Identify areas where it needs to improve
- Plan an improvement programme
- Monitor its progress towards best practice.

Standards can be benchmarked against:

- Competitors
- Organizations in related industries
- Organizations who demonstrate best practice in a generic area such as customer service.

Information for benchmarking can be obtained through a number of channels, including:

- Formal or informal agreements with other organizations to share benchmarking information
- Initiatives by trade associations.

THE POWER OF THE DATABASE

Every company holds a vast reservoir of valuable information, but few tap its power. Database management can help improve your competitive performance through more effective and flexible use of business information. Potentially valuable business information may be locked away in stand-alone departmental systems – transaction details, information on value and frequency of purchase, service records, customer complaints, response to direct mail and telemarketing initiatives, market research information, customer feedback, contact details and customer correspondence. Database management allows you to manage that information more effectively to improve profiling, identify trends and make better-informed decisions.

Database management is used to manipulate very large amounts of data. One American organization has already set up a database which will segment and store information on nearly all consumers in the USA. The database supports the marketing and development of a range of fast-moving consumer products and is used by more than 10 000 users at twenty separate locations.

Database information can be accessed through personal computers and distributed via a network to the people who need it. By streamlining the flow of information through your organization, you can repeatedly identify opportunities and threats faster, and with greater accuracy. By channelling the latent power of information, you can make better and faster decisions, accelerate business advantage and become a more responsive organization.

By coordinating disparate data into focused business intelligence, you can identify new opportunities, enhance customer service and respond to changing market conditions. Take customer service as an example. Customers are demanding greater choice, higher standards of service, and products to match their individual requirements. Understanding and responding to individual needs is vital to survival and profitability, and rapid access to comprehensive, accurate information is the key to optimum performance.

A global retailer operates a worldwide after-sales service for its customers. Database management is used to support service management on a massive scale. The system is able to handle data on:

- 60 million customers
- 17 million service orders
- 4 million parts numbers
- 100 000 service calls a day.

Database management allows the company to manage its service operations more efficiently and deliver an improved standard of service to its customers, wherever they are located.

Customer information unpackages the package holiday

The more you know about your customers, the better you can serve them, as this example from the holiday industry shows. Although the package holiday accounts for an extremely high proportion of holidays, database information is increasingly used to offer customized holiday offers to individuals. A recent advertisement for a frequent-flyer programme demonstrated the potential of database information to customize the offer and strengthen customer relationships. This is the copy taken from an advertisement. The company is able to target the customer so precisely because it has been gathering information on flying patterns and choices and using the database to build a profile of individual customers.

> 'This man flies with us regularly on business. He took a family holiday in Spain during the Barcelona Olympics. His last flight to Munich was during the World Athletic Championships. The promise of a free family ticket to Sydney should keep him loyal to us.'

Another airline uses customer information to make tailored offers and fill empty flights. As an example, they identified flyers who took ski trips and had high points totals. Customers were offered a special ski trip for a low price plus 10 000 collector points. This not only helped to build customer loyalty, it also filled the aeroplane.

CREATING AND USING A DATABASE

A database is the most advanced method of managing and utilizing customer and prospect information. A database holds not only the basic name and address information but also information on prospects which can be refined to provide precise targeting. A database can be run on a personal computer or mainframe computer, depending on size and complexity. Special software is available to manage the information. *The Price Waterhouse Sales and Marketing Software Handbook* (Pitman Professional Publishing, 1993) is a useful guide to the systems currently available.

If you want to set up a database, but do not have the skills within your own organization we recommend consulting either a computer bureau or a direct marketing agency. The information is obtained from customer and prospect records.

A consumer database might include the following information:

Name and address	Marital status
Income level	Occupation category
Home owner/home value	Car owner/car value
Personal interests	Credit card holder

Shopping patterns   Leisure interests
Brand preferences   Recent purchase history
Reading/viewing habits

A business database might include the following information:

Name and address   Type of business
Size of business   Number of employees
Annual expenditure   Average order size
Purchasing frequency   Head office/local purchasing
Purchasing history   Key contacts
Job title   Budget authority

A database can be a powerful tool provided it is used effectively. A database enables you to build a greater understanding of individual customer behaviour so that your customer service programmes are precisely focused.

THE IMPLICATIONS OF DATA PROTECTION

If you maintain personal information about one or more individuals on computer (personal information includes names and addresses) you must register your activities with:

The Data Protection Registrar, Springfield House, Water Lane, Wilmslow, Cheshire SK9 5AF

You must also comply with the requirements of the Data Protection Act. To comply you must:

- Show the nature of the data you hold
- Describe the purpose for which the data are to be used, now and in the future.

An information pack and video is available from:

The Data Protection Registrar, FREEPOST, Wilmslow, Cheshire SK9 5AF

The information pack tells you whether you need to be registered and describes the procedure for registration. If you fail to register, or use the data in ways that fall outside the scope of registration, you are committing a criminal offence and can be prosecuted.

COMPETENCE SELF-ASSESSMENT

1 What sort of customer information does your organization hold?

2 You want to improve the service your department offers to internal customers. What research data are available to support your planning and what other information do you need to find out?

3 Your department is underfunded, constantly criticized and threatened with closure. However, you feel that it performs a vital role and is misunderstood. Outline a research programme to identify with whom you should be communicating and what perception they should hold of you.

4 You are responsible for creating a database that can be used by customer service staff. What sort of information should you include on the database?

5 Describe a programme of events and visits that would enable your organization to find out more about customers' requirements.

6 List the factors that should be included in a survey of customers' attitudes to your department.

7 Prepare a script for a telephone research interview to assess customers' attitudes to your products.

8 Prepare a profile of your most important competitor. Assess the threat to your organization.

9 Describe how you would use benchmarking techniques to improve performance.

10 Prepare a postal questionnaire to assess customer satisfaction with your department.

4 Planning your activities

The earlier chapters have helped you to build a picture of your customers and their requirements. This chapter explains how you can plan your activities to meet those requirements. You will be able to assess your current customer service activities, develop a plan to meet customer requirements and communicate that plan.

ASSESSING YOUR CURRENT PERFORMANCE

The first stage in planning is to assess your current performance. The following checklist outlines the key stages in delivering customer service and briefly describes the actions you should be taking at each stage.

A Pre-sales

1 *Advice and guidance* Do you provide your customers with advice and guidance?
2 *Customer communications* Do you keep your customers fully informed on your products and services?
3 *Consultancy* Do you provide a consultancy service to help your customers assess their needs?
4 *Helplines* Do you provide a helpline so that your customers have easy access to information on your products and services?

B Enquiry and ordering

1 *Product information*   How easy is it for your customers to obtain product information?

2 *Ordering*   How simple are your ordering procedures? Can you simplify them even further?

C Product/service

1 *Opening times*   Are your business hours convenient for your customers? Could you arrange 'out-of-hours' service?

2 *Convenience*   Are your outlets conveniently located? Could you substitute other forms of distribution that are more convenient?

3 *Packaging*   Could you 'package' your products in a different format that makes them easier to use? Could you use new technology such as the Internet to make your products or services more accessible?

4 *Information*   Do you provide full information and documentation to help your customers take full advantage of your products?

5 *Service options*   Do you offer your customers other services to help them benefit from your products?

6 *Quality*   How effective are your quality processes?

7 *Guarantees*   What guarantees do you offer your customers?

8 *Service standards*   Do you have published service standards?

D Purchase administration

1 *Invoicing*   Are your billing processes timely and accurate?

2 *Enquiries*   Do you handle billing and other customer enquiries efficiently?

3 *Documentation*   Do you provide your customers with full and useful documentation?

E Sales follow-up

1 *Follow-up*   Do you make follow-up calls to customers after a sale?

2 *Research*   Do you carry out research into the effectiveness and acceptability of your products or services?

3 *Feedback*   Do you operate a formal feedback process for your customers?

4 *Customer-retention programmes*   Do you operate customer-retention programmes to improve customer loyalty?

F After-sales support

1 *Information helplines*   Do you provide your customers with helplines for follow-up advice?

2 *Maintenance*   Do you offer a maintenance service?

3 *Training*   Do you provide your customers with a training service to help them make effective use of your products?

G Customer service standards

1 *Customer charters*   Do you publish a customer charter?
2 *Customer service standards*   Do you have written customer service standards?
3 *Measurement processes*   Do you have a formal method of measuring your customer service performance?
4 *Awareness of standards*   Are your staff and your customers aware of your customer service standards?
5 *Relationship between standards and improvement programmes*   Do you operate programmes to improve your customer service standards?
6 *Responsibility for managing standards*   Who is responsible for customer service in your organization?

H Customer feedback mechanisms

1 *Customer satisfaction*   Do you have a formal process for measuring customer satisfaction?
2 *Feedback*   What is the frequency of feedback? Do you analyse feedback and respond to it?

I Complaints management

1 *Type of complaints mechanisms*   Do you have a formal mechanism for handling complaints?
2 *Communication to customers*   Are customers aware of the complaints mechanism? Do you encourage complaints?
3 *Response to complaints*   How do you respond to complaints? Do you analyse complaints and use them as the basis for improvements?

J Product/service development

1 *Customer consultation*   Do you consult your customers when you are developing new products or services?
2 *Joint ventures*   Have you considered joint ventures to develop new products?

DEVELOPING A PLAN

This section briefly outlines the key elements of a customer service/marketing plan. It uses information that can be obtained in other sections of this book and provides guidelines so that you can develop your own plan.

Input

What information should you use as input to the plan?

Strategic business plan

Customer service and marketing objectives are derived from overall corporate objectives. Assess your company's strategic business plan to see that customer service and marketing objectives are in line with future direction. Look also at financial objectives to see how marketing actions will contribute.

Research

Customer research, described earlier in Chapter 3, will provide information on the market, your customers, competitors and other factors that affect your ultimate success. Use this information as a basis for planning.

Product plans

Does your company plan to introduce new products, enhance existing ones or phase out declining products? The plan should take account of any likely changes.

Sales records/forecast

What are the sales targets for the whole company and for individual products? What level of sales and marketing expenditure will be needed to achieve these targets?

Customer records

What do customer records indicate about changes in customer markets and the likely impact on demand for the company's products and services? Which customer groups will become important and what actions will be needed to take advantage of the opportunities?

Pricing information

How does competitive pricing affect your own position? What marketing actions will be needed to support changes in pricing?

Competitor information

Competitive actions will have a direct impact on your own plans. Use the information available from competitor research to determine the actions needed to retain and increase market share.

External factors

External factors such as the state of the economy, changes in levels of imports and exports and levels of consumer spending influence your short- and long-term marketing plans. Assess the key factors that influence the success of your business.

CONTRIBUTIONS TO THE PLAN

This section provides guidelines on the people inside and outside your organization who should be consulted about the marketing plan.

Managing director

The managing director and other senior executives provide valuable input about the company's strategic business objectives.

Marketing executives

Marketing executives are directly involved in the formulation of the plan and its implementation. Ask for reviews of current performance and important actions.

Sales executives

Sales executives are in direct contact with customers. They can provide valuable input on customer attitudes and requirements.

Communications specialists

Communications specialists determine the communications strategies needed to achieve marketing objectives.

Product managers

Product managers provide important information on the promotional and communications requirements for new and existing products.

External consultants

External consultants such as management consultants can provide valuable objective input on the company's strategic direction and the marketing options available.

COMMUNICATING THE PLAN

Implementing the plan may involve major change. When a company goes through a major change a clear, consistent, internal communications strategy is vital. Change creates an atmosphere of uncertainty and it is important that everyone understands the major issues and feels that they can contribute to the success of a change. In an atmosphere of uncertainty, customer service levels can be adversely affected. A communications strategy that explains the positive benefits of the change is vital.

Staff briefings, information packs, magazines and other publications describing the rationale for change can all help to build understanding of the new approach. There are also key influencers within the organization – management groups, workteams and key employees who can help to develop a communications channel throughout the organization and spread important messages.

Change is rarely simple and effective communications are essential to ensure that change is handled successfully. Change can be a powerful positive factor rather than a cause for concern and change can demonstrate that an organization is committed to improvement and progress.

Encouraging commitment

Achieving effective changes requires commitment and involvement from all employees. Before implementing a major programme, it is sensible to find what the level of commitment is.

A public utility wanted to encourage greater employee commitment and improve the flow of internal communications in what had been a very hierarchical industry. The company wanted to ensure that employees understood the objectives of the company and identified with them. It carried out an attitude survey anonymously, but decided to publish all the results in a company magazine.

The most important part of the process was the follow-up. Too many employees believed their efforts to complete the survey would be wasted because nothing would happen. The company therefore set up a process for involving employees in improvement programmes.

Communications to build customer focus

Introducing customer focus can have a major impact on many different parts of an organization. Internal communications should be structured to build understanding in all the departments which contribute to customer care. These might include:

- Design
- Manufacturing
- Distribution

- Sales and marketing
- Administration
- Accounts

Many of these departments do not feel that they contribute directly to customer focus, but their role is vital in ensuring overall customer satisfaction. The communications programme begins at the recruitment stage when recruitment advertisements spell out corporate policy on customer care.

Elements in a communications programme

- Recruitment communications
- Training material
- Employee guides
- Motivation and award programmes

Recruitment advertisements and recruitment literature should stress that the company is committed to the highest standards of customer care and that each individual is responsible for achieving corporate standards and contributing to overall corporate success. These recruitment messages can help to build confidence in employees that they have an important role to play in the success of the company and this helps to build awareness and commitment throughout an organization.

Training literature and programmes should also reflect the importance of customer care and explain that training is available to each employee to improve standards. To help employees understand the importance of customer service and the practical implications of customer focus programmes, customer satisfaction guides should be issued to all employees. These describe the main problems faced by customers and explain their main concerns about the service that should be provided. The guide should also describe the most important elements of customer service and the standards which apply.

Motivation and award programmes can help to maintain high levels of interest in the customer focus programme and build a high level of commitment to the programme's success. Programmes like Ford's Chairman's Award for Customer Excellence reward continued improvement in levels of customer satisfaction and give customer service programmes a high profile. They are therefore valuable in building team spirit and a commitment to excellence.

THE KEY TO SUCCESSFUL CHANGE

- Providing a vision
- Leading from the top
- Developing champions

Providing a vision

ICL saw the importance of a vision when they built their quality programme and their internal communications around the concept of the 'ICL Way'. This was a simple phrase, but it formed part of every communication and it implied that every activity had to be a quality activity. The graphic device was simple – a tick – a recognized quality symbol, but sheer weight of use gave it added value and strength.

Ford launched their internal and external communications programme with a vision of total quality that would extend throughout the supply chain. The programme was supported by a vision 'Quality First' which was also used by sub-contractors to put together their own quality programmes. The vision was reinforced by another important factor – the supplier group had been rationalized and the remaining suppliers had to comply with the standards to remain on the approved list.

Leading from the top

When programmes like Total Quality Management have such far-reaching implications, it is essential that the programme is led from the top. ICL's chairman at the time, Peter Bonfield, adopted a high profile during the transformation of ICL to a total quality company. Bonfield led the programme personally – briefing senior management groups, talking to groups of employees, appearing in videos and using every public relations opportunity to raise the profile of the quality programme. Interviews with Bonfield were replayed on the corporate video network and in employee magazines, as well as customer publications. Bonfield put quality on the corporate agenda and demonstrated a personal commitment to its success.

Developing champions

The leader cannot achieve all the communications objectives alone, so it is essential that other people can take on the role of filtering the message through the organization. Management commentators call these people champions. Their task is to utilize communications media to build commitment and enthusiasm for change. Champions make frequent presentations, they hold briefing meetings, they are regular contributors to employee magazines and they take personal responsibility for the motivation and incentive programmes that drive the changes forward.

COMMUNICATING YOUR VISION

A vision or mission statement can be an inspiration or a millstone. A good mission statement can give employees a clear indication of their role and responsibilities, but a poor one sounds empty and unconvincing. The following are some examples:

'To be the most trusted partner of our customers by offering top quality expertise enabling the development and improvement of our customer's business.'

'We will help customers gain business advantage from advanced technology by managing the risk.'

'Every client recommends us.'

Each of the mission statements is focused on the customer and this can form the basis of customer service strategy. The mission statement on its own will tell your employees very little. It simply sets out the overall direction. The text that follows is taken from an employee brochure which describes the implications of the mission statement in more detail. The company has recently undergone far-reaching organizational change and is now operating as a single unit. The brochure is addressed to employees who were normally part of different divisions, located in different countries.

Example of a 'vision brochure'

Over the last few months we have been putting together our vision of the future. We've talked to customers, our partners and, most important, to our people. It's clear that everyone in the company wants to succeed and to succeed together. As individuals, we have already had some remarkable successes but when we look at our combined resources, the future really is exciting.

We can't emphasize too much how important it is for us to work together. We are now one company and together we make a really dynamic force. Historically, we have succeeded in different countries with local customers. Now we are going to integrate those skills and resources to transform ourselves into the leading international player in our sector.

So this is our vision. It's more than words on paper – it's the framework we can all use to build our individual plans. Our strategy for the next five years is to grow a single, profitable, successful business. Your contribution will be critical.

If you look at our customer base we are already working with some of the top names in the business and that's a tremendous achievement. We're starting from a position of real strength and we can talk with confidence to our prospects. Our aim is to be the leading supplier to top companies in our market sector.

First and foremost, we want to grow our business with existing customers and that means a commitment from everyone to first-class customer service. We must share our vision with our customers – every time we meet them, talk to them, or write to them. Let them know that we have a clear view of how we can help them now and in the future. Customers have confidence in a company that knows where it will be in five years' time.

In the long-term we aim to be number one in Europe. The only way we can do that is to present ourselves as a single European business with a consistent reputation. Although we will position ourselves as a significant international business, we must not throw away our local relationships. It's important that we reinforce the values of accessibility with local customers and maintain the quality of 'local service'.

Our future is a 'people business'. Throughout the company, we have quality people with highly developed skills. What we need to do is pull those skills together so that they are available to every customer. A local customer should have access to the best people within the company, wherever they are located. To make the transition, we have put in place an international programme of training, development, redeployment and recruitment. And that, we believe, means exciting and rewarding career opportunities for everyone in the company.

We are moving towards our vision from a position of strength. We have successful national companies and a sound customer base. Most important, we have quality people who are motivated to succeed. We have a clear direction for the future and that direction means that we must think and act as a single team. That is how our customers must see us. Nothing less will do. Please talk to your colleagues and discuss how your individual actions can contribute to the vision. Together we can transform the future.

KEY ELEMENTS OF THE COMMUNICATIONS PROGRAMME

This example of a 'vision brochure' gives the people in the organization a clear sense of direction. It helps them to focus on their responsibilities and their contribution. It also describes what customers should expect in terms of service. The following are the key elements:

The company's overall direction
The customer's expectations
The potential contribution of each employee
The opportunities and benefits for employees
The support available
The timetable for change

PLANNING FOR ACTION

A plan is not an end in itself, but a blueprint for action. Some managers avoid planning because they believe they have more important day-to-day tasks to deal with. Others produce attractive documents which simply sit on the shelf and are never translated into action. Both approaches are wrong. Without effective planning, your day-to-day tasks will lack direction; they will simply be responses to circumstances. Without action, your plans are wasted.

A well-documented plan provides a guideline for other people. It details their responsibilities and shows what they should achieve and when. Just as important, a good plan summarizes the thinking and the conditions behind the plan. If any of those change, the plan can be revised. Above all, planning should help you to meet customer needs more effectively. It focuses the mind of every member of your team on the key tasks needed to improve customer satisfaction.

CHARACTERISTICS OF A GOOD PLAN

Good plans share a number of important characteristics:

- They address the relevant issues.
- They are focused on action and include an action plan.
- They are practical and achievable.
- They incorporate clearly defined objectives.
- They include strategies which can be easily implemented.
- They allocate responsibilities and identify expected results.
- They are measurable.
- They are flexible enough to accommodate change, failure and success.
- They are easily updated or revised.
- They include timings and costings.
- They include a summary of the background to the plan.

THE IMPORTANCE OF ACTION

The action plan is one of the most important elements. It ensures that you achieve results. The plan should include the following elements:

- Action to be taken
- Start date
- Completion date
- Staff responsible
- Methods
- Resource requirements
- Special needs
- Impact

This action plan can be issued as a separate document to the main plan and circulated to everyone involved in the project. The action plan helps to build understanding and awareness, and ensures that there is no misunderstanding.

MONITORING ACTION PLANS

As a manager, you are responsible for ensuring that your staff carry out their responsibilities effectively. Monitoring progress enables you to spot any potential problems and take remedial action before the problem impacts on the success of the whole project. As well as monitoring progress, you should also review progress with your team:

- Hold regular review meetings at key stages of the project.
- Recognize team achievements such as early completion.
- Provide support if team members encounter difficulties in meeting targets.
- Discuss actions to overcome problems and involve the team in any fundamental changes to the plan.

Planning is a dynamic process which takes place in a changing environment. Careful monitoring ensures that you can respond effectively to change.

COMPETENCE SELF-ASSESSMENT

1 Assess the current performance of your department or organization in terms of delivering customer service.
2 Prepare a plan for making a major improvement in the services of your department.
3 What impact will the departmental improvements have on the performance of the organization as a whole?
4 Prepare a list of contributors to the organizational plan and outline the significance of their contribution.
5 Describe the 'vision' for your organization.
6 Prepare a plan for communicating the vision.
7 Identify 'champions' within your organization and describe how you would use them to successfully implement your plan.
8 What organizational changes will your plan require?
9 Prepare a timetable for putting your plan into action.
10 Prepare an agenda for a review meeting to be held at a critical stage of the project. Assume that problems have arisen and you need to get the project back on target.

5 An effective working environment

An effective working environment helps people to make a more effective contribution to customer service. Sharing information, building teams, improving productivity and using technology to enhance personal and organizational performance can all help to improve standards within an organization.

CHANGING CULTURE TO CREATE CUSTOMER FOCUS

Many companies aspire to changing their culture to improve customer focus, but unless the change is managed effectively, the results can be disappointing.

A leading bank launched a fundamental culture change programme with a five-year time span. The aim was to change customers' perception of the branch network from 800 'mini-banks' to branded outlets of a central bank. Research indicated that customers were getting different credit decisions from different branches and an inconsistent service offer. In some extreme cases a branch without a mortgage specialist might have recommended customers contact a building society. Account processing was also fragmented and the net result was described as 'a broken bank'. The bank's ambitions, however, were to be one of the UK's top performers.

The bank identified four key factors for a successful change programme:

A credible vision that is achievable and relevant to customers and staff
A plausible strategy that is capable of delivering the vision
Tangible deliverables and milestones
Measurable progress

Managing change, they believe, is about striking a balance. How much should the bank disclose to employees? How can you give staff a credible view of the future while knowing that vital productivity gains would lead to job losses?

Striking a balance

Managers must be highly visible in a change programme. They must appear at all the key staff meetings and they must speak with a single voice. Any public disagreements about policy can slow down progress. Senior managers must also be honest and allow their own decisions to be questioned.

Open communications are also integral to the process. Staff must hear about change from the management team, not from the press or from the trades union. A planned communications programme is essential, utilizing video, newsletters, team briefings and 'dialogues' which give staff the opportunity to raise questions with a guaranteed response within a certain time.

The bank also emphasized the importance of 'quick wins' to demonstrate that the programme is progressing. However, these must be customer-driven. For example, a clerical incentive scheme included a bonus for imposing charges on customers when a cheque bounced – hardly a customer-focused initiative.

The best change programmes have three elements:

- They begin with a clear vision and strong customer proposition.
- They should be driven by pressures outside the bank.
- It must be a programme and not a series of unrelated initiatives.

RE-ENGINEERING FOR CUSTOMER FOCUS

Business process re-engineering has been used to transform customer service. If the changes are to work, training must be an integral part of the process.

In the early 1990s a major assurance company embarked on a radical programme of business process re-engineering. Starting with a blank sheet of paper, its core business processes were redesigned. Today, the organization is demonstrating measurable improvements in terms of customer satisfaction, reductions in process turnround times of 40–90% and 50–80% quality improvements. The time taken to issue a new policy has been reduced from 46 days to 15.

The key business achievements
Process turnround times down 40–90%
Quality improvements up 50–80%
New policy issue down from 46 to 15 days

Implications for customer service management

The company's success story contains important lessons for customer service management. The company realized that its new business structure ensured that front-line people would have to handle countless new opportunities to serve their customers. It had to ensure that they seized these opportunities.

Business process re-engineering is just half the story. Enabling people to function effectively within their new customer-focused teams is just as critical to success. At the heart of the re-engineering effort was the vision of inverting the old organization structure.

From clerks to case managers

Clerks who used to process paper, never knowing where each form had come from, or where it was going to, would become case managers with full responsibility for seeing the process through from beginning to end and dealing direct with the final customer.

From manager to coach

Their managers, one-time technical experts in the issuing of policies, would be required to pass on their skills to the front-line people. In future, managers' performance would be measured according to how well they inspired their people to deliver outstanding service to customers, rather than on their own personal technical skill and knowledge.

The training task

Having the vision was one thing, breathing life into it quite another. The skills that would be required of those operating at all levels within the new structure had been identified by an intensive process of interviews with a wide cross-section of staff, lasting some 85 hours.

Training was developed to reinforce the importance of front-line people and their managers, not just doing the right things, but also demonstrating the right types of behaviour – listening, innovating, self-checking and team working.

Defining the role of the customer service manager

Each new team participated in a series of workshops before it went live within the new structure. Each team member at every level gave their input to how the team should organize itself to play to the strengths of its members, and what percentage of time should be focused on which accountability.

Managers who thought that they could get away with spending 80% of their time living in the old world and focusing on technical matters were soon put right by their team members. The team demanded that the managers should take their role as performance managers and coaches very seriously. Those who couldn't or wouldn't had to find new roles and make way for others to assume the key position of customer service manager.

Monitoring the process

A comprehensive audit process to assess the results of the work confirmed its effectiveness. The following quotation captures the effort and creativity with which the whole enterprise was approached by everyone involved:

'Coming to work now isn't just mechanical; it has become a process of developing yourself, cooperating with others, flexibility and enhancing the way you work.'

A continuous process

The process has not ended and, according to the company, it is unlikely that it will. But the company believes that, unless they had exposed their managers to the full implications of what the new structure really means, they might never have taken those important first steps.

Key elements in the transformation
Measurable business improvements
Inverting traditional structures
Empowering front-line staff
Supporting front-line staff with training and development
Giving managers responsibility for coaching

Identifying and improving the key behavioural competencies
Monitoring progress
Treating change as a continuous process

TEAM WORKING BOOSTS CUSTOMER SATISFACTION

Team working and multi-skilling is increasingly discussed in the context of manufacturing. It also offers potential benefits for customer service, as a Japanese hotel demonstrates.

Tokyo's Daiichi Hotel Annex, where team working has been successfully introduced, was voted number one in a recent customer-satisfaction survey. Hotel staff are divided into three teams:

- Room related
- Eating and drinking
- Cooking

Within each team, staff cover all specific job functions. For example, within the room-related team, the concierge, bell-boy and receptionist cover for each other at busy times, or when something unusual occurs. The company training manual compares this approach to that of a successful baseball team where players combine specialist skills with support for other team members.

Key points from the Daiichi Hotel experience

Team working can make an important contribution to customer satisfaction
Multi-skilling can be used to improve service levels
Good team members support each other in busy periods

VIDEOCONFERENCING CUTS TRAVEL AND IMPROVES PERFORMANCE

If you spend a lot of time travelling to meetings on other company sites or with suppliers, it's worth looking at the benefits of videoconferencing. Meetings are essential, travel isn't. It wastes time and puts a strain on people. Checking diaries inevitably pushes meetings back. Decisions are delayed, projects miss their targets. That's good news for competitors.

A new generation of desktop systems now makes videoconferencing affordable and easy to use. A single card, installed in a single personal computer slot, converts a PC into a complete communications workstation. Through their PCs, people can hear and see colleagues face-to-face, wherever they are in the world, and exchange and amend documents and graphics on the screen.

Bringing people together

Videoconferencing is an ideal alternative for meetings with suppliers, as well as colleagues working in other locations or away from the office. Video-conferencing improves communications, increases efficiency and saves valuable travelling time and costs. It also increases contact, improves working relation-ships and builds vital team spirit. Working together with videoconferencing is just like holding a meeting – people can judge their colleagues' reactions, review information together and reach decisions quickly.

Management meetings

Videoconferencing helps to reduce the time and improve the value of meetings. Sales managers can hold more frequent reviews with branch managers and district sales teams; marketing executives can liaise more easily with product managers or other specialists in different locations, and any group of senior executives can hold urgent meetings immediately.

Cut travel costs

Why condemn your best people to days on the road, in planes or in hotels? It costs them valuable time and it costs you money. In short, it's unproductive, expensive and frustrating. Flying people to meetings in Europe several times a month used to cost one manufacturer around £300 000 a year. They've halved that by using videoconferencing.

Project management

Videoconferencing is ideal for review meetings that don't require face-to-face contact – reviewing proposals, discussing progress, or modifying schedules. By establishing videoconferencing links with colleagues and suppliers, you can streamline many of the processes of project management.

Access to remote expertise

In businesses such as retailing, banking, local government and many other industries, companies need to provide complex multiple services to their customers, often from many different sites. Experts cannot be available in all these places, but videoconferencing allows them to be consulted quickly and easily, via a screen, wherever they are located.

Improve customer service

Help desks are essential to giving customers access to service staff. Videoconferencing provides a friendly, efficient form of help that can improve customer satisfaction.

Integrated audio, video and data communications

With videoconferencing, people can communicate in three dimensions – audio, video and data. A desktop camera permits face-to-face contact and, in addition, pre-recorded videos can be transmitted. Files containing text and graphics can be transferred at high speeds to colleagues in advance of a meeting, while documents can be sent across the link during a meeting for review and annotation by other participants.

An integral 'whiteboard' allows participants to call up a document and share it. Each participant can annotate relevant sections or note changes, while others can introduce their own documents using the whiteboard. This facility can also be used to support joint creation of documents, diagrams or drawings during a meeting and each participant can save their own annotated version of a new document.

Make better decisions, faster

Videoconferencing is easy to use with simple, user-friendly controls and it doesn't just bring people together. If you're making decisions about policies, products, or projects – anything that involves written or graphic images – videoconferencing allows you to exchange data and make and review changes during the meeting – quickly and easily.

Developing videoconferencing skills

Simply investing in videoconferencing equipment does not improve communications, it is important to develop the right skills to take full advantage of the medium. About one third of our ideas are communicated through sound, but two thirds are communicated through sight. 'That', according to a consultant, 'makes PC videoconferencing one of the most exciting technology opportunities for managers and professionals since the invention of the telephone. Many of the subtle techniques we use naturally to communicate face-to-face are missing when we use the telephone. Take eye contact, hand movement, posture and facial expressions – you simply can't reproduce them over the telephone. There are about 3000 words available for instant recall in our vocabulary, yet all of us have over 20 000 discernibly different facial expressions.'

It is important for people to learn how to share and manipulate information in a new way. PC videoconferencing requires skills in team working, delegation, negotiation and presentation. It's vital that people develop natural, visible confidence.

VIRTUAL ORGANIZATIONS PUT SKILLS IN THE RIGHT PLACE

The concept of a virtual organization may sound futuristic, but it is already a reality and it is helping companies improve their marketing edge. A European software company with operations in five countries uses the 'virtual team' approach to deliver a consistent standard of service to customers wherever they are located. Specialists can be based in any country but their skills are available to other countries thanks to a 'knowledge network' and modern tele-communications. According to the company, the knowledge network is a framework for ensuring consistent delivery of value to its customers and it depends on two key elements – a cooperative team structure and an infrastructure to support the development, sharing and re-use of a combined base of experience.

'The quality of our people is crucial to the success of the programme. Our people are members of a team: each has a specialism and most are likely to be leaders in their field; some will be the sponsors of a method or a technology, and others will engineer success time after time. What they have in common is that they are catalysts for our customers' businesses and channels for delivering the knowledge and experience of the whole team.'

To make the most of their combined skills and experience, the company has created a knowledge network which has four major elements:

- *Experts* – the people themselves who bring industry-leading levels of expertise and experience
- *Knowledge database* – the knowledge database provides a flexible platform for the storage, organization and retrieval of the company's expertise and experience
- *Knowledge network* – all the staff have access to the knowledgebase, wherever they are located

■   *Methodology* – the database provides a responsive frame-work to guide the successful use and re-use of our combined expertise and experience and gives the teams immediate access to pools of experience from similar assignments.

The knowledge environment is continually enhanced and extended to ensure that the company's teams are backed by a wide range of current information which can be practically applied to business situations. The knowledge environment allows the company to operate as a virtual organization. It has developed centres of expertise across Europe where people focus on particular areas of expertise. However, through networking and the knowledge environment, the company can create virtual teams with the most appropriate skills. The result is a highly practical solution that gives customers access to the full resources of the group, wherever they are located.

ENHANCING CUSTOMER SERVICE THROUGH FLEXIBLE WORKING

Flexibility is key to building efficiency and competitiveness. It increases productivity and reduces costs, enhances the quality of service, improves employee relations and ensures a better alignment of skills to market needs.

Achieving flexibility means making the best use of your people through new working practices such as team working, work groups, use of external contractors/specialists and part-time working. It also means tailoring your organization to your people through location-independent working, 'hot-desking', teleworking and working 'on the move'.

These changes have far-reaching implications for internal and external communications. You have to provide all your users with access to effective communications, wherever and whenever they need them. The simple 'desk-bound' phone is no longer appropriate – a new solution is needed.

'Flexible office' solutions, available from telecommunications suppliers, allow you to support flexible working by customizing your communications to match your preferred business process. They link together communications and computer networks to simplify access to multiple technologies such as voice, fax and electronic mail. They improve office communications and increase productivity.

Keeping team communications in control

One company found that, on an average day, 10% of their customer-facing staff would be away from their desks. They decided to implement 'hot desking', with staff sharing desks and work areas as necessary. A flexible office solution is used to manage all telephone calls, allowing staff to work at any location without affecting communications. Calls can be routed to any desk, to voicemail or to a paging system. This ensures optimum use of space and enhances caller service. It also ensures that customers can always reach key staff when they call.

Keeping in touch with the salesforce

Flexible, effective communications are essential to the success of a field salesforce, who might only visit their office occasionally. A flexible office solution helps maintain high levels of contact at all times. To reach an individual representative, customers always call just one number and the call is automatically routed to the most appropriate destination. Calls can be routed to car phones, a secretary, voicemail, the representative's home or the sales support team. If the first choice is unavailable or doesn't answer, automatic call management tries alternative destinations so that no call goes unanswered.

Location-independent working

If your customer-facing staff need the flexibility to move freely around a site or if they do not have a permanent desk, call routing is no longer a problem. Users who work from home or who travel frequently can also be reached easily. Flexible office solutions automatically route calls to individuals, link into voicemail or divert calls to nominated colleagues. It also supports the integration of complementary technologies to provide PC video facilities and remote data access. Users inform the system of their location by entering a personal identification number at their nearest telephone or by selecting from a menu of options on their PC.

Working on the move

It's vital to maintain contact when key customer-facing staff are working off-site. Even with mobile telephones, communications can still be difficult. Flexible office solutions increase the number of options available for call handling and message management. Users can arrange to have calls diverted to colleagues, routed to mobile phones, pagers or home numbers, or stored in voicemail.

Supporting work groups

Many organizations are bringing their customer-facing staff together in teams or work groups to focus the right skills on a specific project or on a service such as accounts, customer service or sales. Flexible office solutions improve the efficiency of internal and external communications by ensuring that all calls will be answered, whether individual team members are on-site or not. For example, a 'team call' facility, where the phone number relates to the service instead of a named individual, means callers can be routed to the most suitable member of the team. Team members' calls are routed to their current locations, irrespective of where they are working. This allows teams to be split across sites or to work from home and there is no limit to team size.

Components of the flexible office

Flexible office solutions bring together data processing, voice and data communications applications in an integrated solution that need not require a major investment in new telephone systems. They build on your existing telecommunications and data infrastructure and are fully compatible with modern telephone systems and personal computer networks. A flexible office solution might include:

- *Intelligent telephony services* – computer-based applications that fully integrate with a telephone system to provide routing of voice and fax calls to an individual or team, regardless of location
- *Messaging and voice processing* – message management and call processing systems that help you communicate more effectively, both internally and externally, with the potential to increase productivity and reduce call-handling costs
- *Desktop* – software applications running on personal computers that integrate voice, fax and e-mail in a Windows environment. When combined with Intelligent Telephony Services, Desktop also allows users to control routing of their incoming calls and make outgoing calls from their PC
- *Personal videoconferencing* – a single card, installed in a single PC slot, that provides worldwide video and data conferencing from any location connected to the global ISDN communications network

---

Flexible   office: improving   the   quality   of communications
- Voice, fax and data communication is available to users, wherever they are
- No calls are lost
- People are more accessible
- Calls can be automatically routed to the right 'service area', rather than named individuals
- Callers get a quicker response

DIRECT APPROACH IMPROVES CUSTOMER SERVICE

A regional bank wanted to increase sales of personal loans in the highly competitive UK market through faster response, enhanced customer service and greater flexibility. To support this, the bank has set up a 'direct' telephone operation and is utilizing computerized workflow techniques to streamline the processing of loan applications. The bank has already reduced loan completion by several days.

To help meet its objectives of increasing the volume, value and quality of its loans business, the bank carried out a preliminary study into the loan-application process, and a telephone-based system was identified as the key to success. The bank originally handled personal loan applications by post – a time-consuming process that occupied a large team working with separate IT systems. The telephone-based service enables the bank to focus its expertise in selling financial services and increase market penetration without extending the branch network. It also enhances the quality of service to customers and increases productivity. Customers now enjoy the flexibility and convenience of a telephone service that has made the 'direct' approach so popular in financial services.

The first stage of the project has already seen important benefits – customer service levels are up, the loan turnaround time has been drastically reduced, and it takes just less than half the original number of people to process a higher number of applications. The improved effectiveness of the loan process is helping the bank increase its customer base through quality customer service and the bank is so confident that it is now expanding the operation to further accelerate the growth plan.

A valuable aspect of the project was the opportunity for input from different groups within the bank – including the main board, marketing, credit control, users and the IT department. The solution balanced the requirements of different groups and provided an opportunity to resolve any conflicts of priority between the groups. The review helped to identify the key business and customer service issues and ensured that they were reflected in the solution.

Faster decisions

It used to take about an hour to approve a loan in principle and seven days to complete a loan. Integrating the bank's credit-scoring system to provide on-line credit assessment has reduced the average to twelve minutes for an approval in principle and only three days to complete. The loan can now be approved in principle on the first call and that has a significant effect on customer satisfaction.

Improved customer care

Since individual customer loan details are held on the system, customers can now speak to any of the team to discuss their loan. There is no delay and no need for a return call because all operators have instant access to the loan history. The number of phone calls from customers inquiring about their loan status has dropped by 90%.

Personal relationship with the customer

Operators enjoy a wider, more positive role. Instead of just taking details of a loan application over the phone and passing it to a different work area, they can now deal with the customer personally and give the customer an immediate response. They also have the opportunity to build greater rapport and sell additional related products such as loan insurance.

Freeing staff for more skilled work

The customer service systems is fully integrated with the bank's database systems, allowing accounts to be created and tracked for the period of the loan and supplying vital management information on customers. The complete process has been streamlined and staff have full access to supporting information. They can now track customer loan cases easily and automate routine responses so that they can concentrate on skilled work and develop customer relationships.

More business with the same people

The bank is increasing its customer base rapidly and winning new business in a fiercely competitive market. Thanks to the workflow solution staff can handle much higher volumes of loan applications, with no reduction in service levels. During the first year of implementation, the monthly volume of personal loan applications handled by the bank has increased dramatically, while numbers of customer service staff have remained stable.

The customer service system has achieved its original objective of speeding up the processing of loan applications. The bank has now developed a reputation for responsive, high-quality customer service and that is helping it to expand its customer base even further.

BETTER ACCESS TO COMPANY INFORMATION IMPROVES CUSTOMER SERVICE

Over 90% of business information is still held in paper form. It's easy to read and cheap to produce, but it holds back real freedom of information.

Freedom of information means quick, easy access, rapid distribution, simple low-cost storage and high levels of security, and the results can be measured in improved customer service and greater productivity. Effective customer service and marketing relies on information, but so much of that information is held in departmental filing systems that are inaccessible to other departments.

Electronic filing system can now store some 13 000 A4 pages on a disk that fits in the palm of the hand. Microfilm systems are capable of storing 3 million documents in less than a square metre of valuable office space, yet providing access to any one of those documents in seconds. Both approaches will overcome the shortcomings of traditional paper-based filing systems, turning passive storage into active information management:

- Improving customer service by giving sales and marketing staff rapid easy access to information
- Increasing productivity by speeding up file search and response times
- Saving space and money by converting bulky files to compact desktop systems
- Improving security by controlling document access, back-up and distribution
- Reducing the risk of lost or missing documents

IMPROVE EFFICIENCY WITH DOCUMENT MANAGEMENT

Information is one of the most important corporate assets but, to unlock its real value, you need to ensure that it can be easily retrieved, managed and shared. Marketing and customer service activities increasingly depend on quality of information and a document management system could be the answer. Document management ensures that information and documents are available to the right people, whenever they need them, and wherever they are located.

Documents and other forms of information are scanned and converted to electronic form. From a workstation, users can retrieve documents rapidly, review or annotate them, communicate them to other people for comment or approval, and incorporate the information into other popular business applications.

Scope of document management

The term 'document' is increasingly used as a generic one for anything which delivers information. It can exist in many forms:

- Customer letters
- Sales documents
- Faxes
- E-mail
- Press cuttings
- Books
- Reports
- Microfilm
- Digital images
- 35 mm slides
- Audio tapes
- Videos

All these elements can be brought together as one record in the form of a single electronic document or as individual records. The various elements can be scanned or viewed as required.

Why manage your documents?

Whenever this type of material has to be shared, re-used or updated, problems can occur – locating documents, providing documents for multiple use, ensuring that the latest version is used, avoiding bottlenecks that impact on customer service, dealing with loss or damage, controlling access to confidential or sensitive information.

Managing your documents electronically has a number of important marketing and customer service benefits:

- Improved access to information
- Faster document retrieval
- Improved response to internal or external queries
- Enhanced decision support
- Support for team-working
- Streamlined administration
- Enhanced customer service
- Improved documentation quality.

Document management checklist

This checklist is designed to help you assess the contribution document management could make to your activities:

1   Document management is ideal for improving the efficiency and productivity of high-volume activities. Which of these is most important to your organization?
    Customer service correspondence
    Publications
    Product information

2   To calculate the potential cost/benefits, it is worth focusing on critical activities:
    Which activity do you feel would benefit most from document management?
    How many users would be involved?
    What is the approximate volume of documents per week/month?
    What are the current storage requirements for this activity?

3   Document management can be used to create electronic documents from a variety of source materials. Which of these items is your main source material?

Letters	Invoices
Purchase orders	Delivery notes
Faxes	E-mail
Press cuttings	Books
Reports	Drawings
Microfilm	Digital images
35 mm slides	Audio tapes
Videos	

4   Documents can be easily shared between different users and departments. Which of these working patterns are important to you?

Workflow	Team working
Parallel working	Simultaneous engineering
Supplier/sub-contractor partnerships	Multiple sites

5   Document management solutions can be integrated with line of business applications and other information systems. What type of integration is important to you?

Corporate network	Mobile data
Word processing	Accounts
Project management	Database management

COMPETENCE SELF-ASSESSMENT

1 Describe how you would introduce team working to your department. How would this benefit customer service?

2 Prepare a plan for re-engineering key customer-facing processes.

3 How could you and your organization make use of videoconferencing?

4 Describe how you could utilize the concept of a virtual organization to enhance service.

5 Prepare a plan for introducing workflow techniques to important customer service processes.

6 Describe how you would communicate the importance of culture change in the organization.

7 Prepare a plan for introducing document management.

8 Describe how flexible working could be used to improve customer service.

9 Could you implement a 'direct' approach in your business? Describe the organizational implications.

10 Describe the most important new technologies for your organization. Assess their impact on customer service.

6 The extended organization

Good customer service goes beyond your own organization. The relationship your organization has with suppliers, retailers, distributors and other members of the 'demand chain' will have an important effect on the service your customers enjoy. You need to ensure that everyone in the demand chain is capable of delivering a quality service through training, information, support and a shared commitment to the customer. As the following list shows, a good working relationship between your organization and your suppliers and retailers can produce outstanding results:

- Innovation
- Better performance
- Lower manufacturing costs
- Reduced operating costs
- Improved whole-life costs
- Development of complete solutions
- Better understanding of customer requirements
- New ways of working together
- High levels of cooperation

WORKING WITH SUPPLIERS

In selecting a supplier, your purchasing policy should be governed by a number of important guidelines:

- To establish partnership with suppliers based on trust and mutual benefit
- To increase the level of cooperation with suppliers to improve reliability, quality and delivery
- To improve your own products and services through cooperation.
- To reduce time to market by speeding up the new-product development process
- To improve competitiveness by reducing costs
- To achieve a better flow of information between manufacturer and suppliers
- To achieve agreement about costs, quality and timescales
- To reduce costs through a process of continuous improvement

Selection criteria

Choosing the right partner is essential and it is important to develop a formal procedure for selecting and evaluating suppliers. It includes the following elements:

- Technical capabilities and resources
- Financial performance
- Delivery reliability
- Quality
- Performance and reputation.

PARTNERSHIP STRENGTHENS THE CUSTOMER SERVICE CHAIN

A new concept in manufacturer–customer relationships is helping to redefine the way companies do business. Demand chain management, unlike traditional supply chain management, begins with the customer and creates a demand-driven environment. To the manufacturer, the competitive edge is derived from the way in which the product is supplied to the market. Demand chain management provides a number of important benefits:

- Quality customer service
- Products tailored to meet the demands of individual customers
- Marketing and pricing fine-tuned to local market conditions
- Cycle times optimized
- Inventory minimized
- Greater flexibility in sourcing, supply and service.

The demand chain can be extremely complex, with many different organizations between the manufacturer or assembler and consumer, including:

- Distributors
- Retailers
- Individual retail branches

From the manufacturer, the chain stretches further back to sub-assembler and component manufacturer. The RSA inquiry 'Tomorrow's Company', has highlighted the importance of the 'inclusive company' which puts a value on all its stakeholders, including employees, suppliers and distributors. This cooperation throughout the demand chain is essential if a company is to deliver the highest levels of customer satisfaction.

In tomorrow's company, relationships will be the underlying source of competitiveness. Successful companies will value and learn from partnerships with all of the stakeholders involved – employees, customers, suppliers, investors and the community. That makes suppliers, employees and retailers an essential part of the company, contributing to overall customer satisfaction. The report cites Unipart, an automotive parts specialist, as a good example of the 'inclusive company'.

Employee development is seen as a key element of the company's long-term strategy, so much so that the company has set up its own university. Here people can improve job skills, develop other personal skills and study subjects of their own interest as part of an overall personal development programme. Other commentators point to the value of well-motivated people who contribute to a more positive interface with the customer.

Relationships with suppliers are also important. In Unipart, suppliers co-operate in 'stakeholder circles' to solve quality problems and participate in a continuous improvement programme called 'Ten-to-Zero' which aims at reducing delivery errors, transaction costs and lead times. Supporters of the inclusive company recommend that companies should share information with their suppliers, set joint target costs and work together to reduce time to market. They encourage suppliers to take the long-term view.

SHARING INFORMATION

Successful demand chain management depends on partnership based on effective information flow throughout the chain:

- Information systems ensure a timely, accurate information flow up the chain from consumer to source
- This supports the planning and execution of that demand so that the 'down' chain from raw material vendor to consumer works as a single, efficient whole

- Special software is used to integrate the management of information from order processing, logistics/manufacturing and customer service operations, making the information easily accessible throughout the life cycle of a customer order
- The whole system is pulled by consumer demand, in sharp contrast to traditional systems which have evolved from order capture or manufacturing control systems.

The key to success is the 'extended enterprise' where the efficient and profitable supply of goods and services depends on cooperation with many partners, and the customer forms an integral part of the enterprise.

An international computer manufacturer markets every type of product from consumables to mainframes, as well as a broad range of professional services. It markets these products in almost every part of the world through channels as diverse as direct telesales, resellers and a direct salesforce. The cycle times range from immediate telesales to complete build-to-order systems.

The company is utilizing a pilot project to assess the implications of an evolution to demand chain management. As part of the evolutionary process, the company is developing partnerships with suppliers and sub-contractors who can provide the sub-assemblies or even custom build a system to meet a specific customer order quickly and cost effectively. The company's role becomes one of design, followed by demand and supply chain management.

The programme uses special software to provide the capability for:

- Inventory control
- Order and purchase management
- Warehouse management
- Supply chain replenishment
- Electronic commerce
- Customer service activities
- Customer and product profiling
- Pricing
- Promotional control.

The company's experience demonstrates the power of demand chain management to transform a business by focusing on customers and reducing costs. It can decrease cycle times, reduce redundant administrative effort, increase flexibility, and is driven by customer needs. Competitive advantage is built on clear customer focus.

EXTENDING THE ENTERPRISE

With the growth of Internet technologies, many companies are looking ahead to see how they can extend their information systems so that they can communicate quickly and effectively outside the organization with customers and distributors. Speed of communication is critical in any business and companies are currently reviewing the potential of Internet and Intranet solutions.

The local knowledge of distributors is extremely valuable and organizations want to enhance their performance by providing them with remote access to their own information systems. The Internet will also help to communicate service information efficiently, perhaps using a web site with restricted access to 'post' service bulletins and deliver 'added-value services'. In the longer term, companies are considering ways to communicate with their customers in the same way, enhancing communications and strengthening customer relationships.

IMPROVING LOCAL PERFORMANCE THROUGH DISTRIBUTOR PARTNERSHIPS

Success in local markets may depend on a good working relationship between a manufacturer and local distributors or retailers. The relationship will improve even more when the two work in partnership. This partnership should be mutually beneficial and it should provide each party with access to scarce skills and resources that would otherwise involve considerable investment.

Using partnership to provide nationwide resources

An engineering company has an established network of distributors, providing different levels of parts and service support to customers. In the past, the engineering company has provided service and maintenance to major customers directly through a small in-house team and has provided a spare-parts service to major customers' own service teams through the distributor network. The distributor service staff provided service and maintenance to other smaller customers or may have provided emergency cover to major customers' in-house teams.

However, an increasing number of major customers are disbanding their own service teams and outsourcing. If the company is to retain contact with these major customers and not lose control to third-party service organizations, it needs to provide nationwide cover, but it does not have the resources. It has a number of choices:

1   Set up their own service network, involving a major investment in service infrastructure and skills
2   Use the service of an independent service organization on a third-party basis
3   Work in partnership with an independent service organization to establish a joint service network conforming to the supplier's quality standards

The manufacturers decide that the distributor service network provides a good basis for the service programme and sets up a partnership agreement with the distributors.

Supporting the distributor

To ensure that customers get the right level of service throughout the network, the manufacturer agrees to support the distributors in the following way:

- Provide full product training for the service staff
- Give full technical support to the service staff
- Provide access to the company's service database
- Develop service tools to enable the distributor service staff to handle more complex service tasks
- Set up simplified ordering procedures so that service staff quickly get the parts they need
- Develop quality standards in conjunction with distributor staff so that the service is delivered to an agreed standard
- Set up a central service reception facility so that customers can easily contact the appropriate service centre to get service anywhere in the country
- Communicate the nationwide service network to their customers

The distributor's commitment

These actions enable the distributors to improve the performance of their own service operations and to provide the level of service needed by the manufacturer. The distributors, for their part, would agree to the following actions:

- Participate in the manufacturer's training programme
- Conform to quality standards that were jointly agreed
- Maintain adequate stock levels to provide adequate service cover
- Give priority to the company's service business
- Comply with response levels

Benefits of the arrangement

The partnership agreement benefits both parties. The manufacturer acquires a quality nationwide service network with the minimum investment and is able to provide a high level of service to customers. The distributors improve their own service performance and gain access to additional sources of service business.

Winning new business through joint ventures

An international engineering group worked with a selected group of engineering distributors in the UK to help them win a major parts and service contract with a major public organization. The distributors had a network of branches strategically located near each of the customer's main depots; they had the product range to meet the customer's demands and their staff were already dealing with the customer on *ad hoc* purchases.

To make an effective pitch for the business, the distributors needed to strengthen their business in a number of areas:

- Scheduled, guaranteed delivery without major stockholding
- Technical support and back-up
- Availability of special products
- Competitive prices on high-volume purchases
- Emergency supply service to keep the customer operations running

The manufacturer was able to provide the continuity of supply and the back-up the distributors needed by analysing the customer's scheduled and emergency stock requirements and developing supply schedules which would enable the distributors to provide guaranteed cover in a cost-effective way.

The partnership arrangement benefited both parties because the manufacturer was able to increase its business with the distributor without the cost of setting up a supply network to service a large multi-site customer and the distributors were able to build on their existing local relationship with the customer to increase their business and secure a major contract.

Identifying partnership opportunities

How could you and your distributors benefit from working more closely together?

1 Can you use your distributors' skills and resources to extend your own services?
2 What would your distributors bring you by working more closely with you and what could you offer them?
3 What type of opportunities could they exploit by working more closely with you?
4 What special service could you offer your distributors in return for greater cooperation?

Keeping distributors involved and motivated

To make a distributor network operate effectively, it is essential to maintain contact with local outlets. How many times has the local office accused head office of being remote and out of touch? Can head office staff be certain that local outlets are aware of the latest product information or the current operating policy? Is there a feeling that certain outlets are better informed or supported than others?

Formal and informal information channels are used to maintain effective contact with local staff at all levels and, as part of the planning process, you should be concerned with developing a contact strategy to meet the following objectives:

- Local managers understand your current business objectives.
- Managers understand their responsibilities and objectives.
- Managers understand corporate operating procedures.
- Managers are aware of the business and marketing support available to their outlet.
- Managers are committed to success.
- Staff understand the relationship between the local outlet and head office.
- Staff have up-to-date product knowledge and understand how to implement company policies.
- Staff feel that they have a worthwhile career structure within the organization.

Within those overall objectives, there may be more specific objectives that are relevant to your network, but the main principles are:

Keep local staff and management fully informed.
Use communications to motivate them to succeed.

IMPROVING RETAIL CONTROL

A major UK brewing group, with over 4000 outlets, is using a central retailing system to improve standards of service in its local outlets. The system collects retail sales data nightly from all the group's outlets, analysing and validating it for control and compliance purposes. As well as communicating with all outlets, it will be available to more than 300 users, and provides the information needed to fine-tune local performance.

The information used by outlet managers, business managers and product/brand managers, as well as functional managers in sales, marketing, finance and operations to supports key functions such as:

- Communicating product and price changes
- Managing product allocation
- Assessing the impact of sales and marketing campaigns

- Releasing new menus and ordering information
- Analysis of outlet and overall performance
- Measurement against performance targets

Business intelligence like this gives the group control, flexibility and the ability to respond rapidly to changes in the marketplace.

IMPROVING CUSTOMER SERVICE THROUGH PRODUCT TRAINING

In today's competitive market, the key to success is quality customer service. Customers increasingly demand more information so it is vital that sales staff are trained to the highest standards. A distance-learning programme is helping sales staff in a national retail group to develop better product knowledge through dedicated product training and support. It has the following objectives:

- Contribute to high levels of customer satisfaction
- Make the company the preferred choice for car buyers
- Focus sales staff attention on customer requirements
- Improve the company's competitive position
- Support the effective launch of new products.

A wide spread of media are used including printed material, audio tapes, videos. New products, specification improvements, prices and competitive actions are all covered. The programme recognizes differing levels of expertise and experience, providing sufficient information to appeal to new salespeople as well as fully experienced individuals. All communications adopt an easy to understand, user-friendly format.

The programme enables vital information on new products to be released immediately and allows information to be updated regularly. Individuals can study at their own pace and the programme can be developed and delivered cost-effectively. The programme's effectiveness is continually monitored through regular quiz competitions. The quality of entries from sales staff is an excellent indicator of their understanding of the material. Sales staff have the opportunity to improve their own product knowledge, but extra motivation is applied in the form of awards which can be achieved by top-scoring sales staff.

The programme has been operating in its present format for 3 years and around 90% of the salesforce currently participate. It is designed for practical day-to-day use, with research indicating that the training material is used five or six times a day in the average retail outlet. The main organizational benefits are:

- Higher levels of customer satisfaction with the sales process

- The retail group is the preferred choice by a higher percentage of buyers
- Sales staff are focused on customer requirements
- The company's competitive position in the marketplace has improved
- New product launches have been more effective.

There have been important benefits to retail branches:

- They are continuing to improve their own levels of customer satisfaction.
- They are able to offer higher standards of customer care.
- They develop highly professional sales teams.
- They can bring new recruits up to speed quickly.
- They make effective use of salesforce time and resources.

Individual sales executives benefit significantly from the programme:

- They are able to improve their product knowledge and keep up to date with product changes.
- They are able to deliver an improved level of care to their customers.
- They can undertake training at their own pace and in their own time so that they can concentrate on delivering customer satisfaction.
- Job satisfaction is increased.

SETTING OUT THE PRINCIPLES OF A SUPPLIER/DEALER RELATIONSHIP

A manual can help to clarify the relationship between manufacturer and dealer. It not only sets out the contractual requirements, it also includes all the information needed to explain the business relationship between a company and its dealers and helps the dealer to run the business effectively. The following example illustrates the type of information that should be included and can be used as a template to develop your own manual. We have included a combination of sample text and contents.

Introduction

We recognize the importance of the flexibility and sales effectiveness that our dealers can provide in the marketplace. We want to strengthen our dealer business even further and we hope that you might be interested in joining the network. In this brochure, we explain the concept of the dealer programme and describe the support available to our dealers. We believe that it provides the basis for joint market success and we look forward to close constructive cooperation.

Profile of the company

This section should include information about the company including:

- Brief history
- Mission
- Organization and structure
- Ownership
- Size, turnover and profitability
- Product range
- Brand names
- Main markets and market position
- Key contacts for dealers

The role of dealers

Dealer business is the key to success in the changing structure of our market. With a growing number of competitors in the small and medium sector, we place increasing importance on the flexibility and sales effectiveness dealers can provide. Forecasts suggest that by 2000, the percentage of business sold through dealers will increase to 40%, up 15% over a ten-year period.

The dealer programme is a key element in our marketing strategy and we are continuing to broaden the range of products and services available to our dealers. With the strength and support of two of the world's leading companies, that means a major competitive advantage for you as a dealer.

The dealer network

We supply a range of products through a number of carefully selected dealers to help us maintain our position in the rapidly changing UK market. Our key objectives are to:

- Establish the company as the UK's leading supplier in its sector through the dealer network
- Increase our joint market share
- Provide the highest level of support to our dealers.

The UK market

The market for our products is forecast to continue as customers demand new features and new solutions that enable them to take advantage of emerging technologies and new services available from manufacturers.

Dealer product strategy

To meet changing customer requirements, we are providing our dealers with a range of innovative products and the highest levels of support. The strength of the parent companies and our commitment to product development ensures that existing products are continually enhanced and new market-leading products are available. Our dealer product strategy will therefore be to:

- Continue to exploit the market leadership of existing products
- Complement the product portfolio by launching new world-class products

Dealer support structure

Support for our dealers falls into four main areas:

- Sales
- Marketing
- Technical
- Commercial

We also ensure that you can deliver the right level of service by participation in our dealer accreditation scheme.

Dealer accreditation

The overall aim of our accreditation scheme is to achieve the objective of growth in partnership with your customers by delivering the highest levels of quality and customer satisfaction. The key elements of the scheme include:

- Sales accreditation
- Technical accreditation
- Commercial accreditation

In each area you and your staff will receive extensive training and support so that you can deliver the highest standards of service across all customer-facing activities. Sales training, for example, ensures familiarity with the range of products and includes guidelines on business conduct and handling customer queries. The technical accreditation programme ensures that your engineers have the product knowledge, tools and skills to install and maintain our products to the highest standards.

Sales support

You deal directly with our dealership marketing team who help with business planning, sales and product training, as well as customer demonstrations for accredited dealers. You will receive sales enquiries which take into account your size, location and performance. In certain cases, we may also be able to introduce accredited dealers to some of our larger accounts or to our service base when replacement systems are required.

The dealership marketing team forms an important link between you and the company. They maintain regular contact with you to keep you up to date with new products and company developments and help you to achieve mutual sales objectives. Their key responsibilities include:

- Selection and authorization of dealers
- Development of dealership structure and qualifications
- Market and customer analysis
- Implementation of mutual sales objectives
- Development of sales and marketing plans
- Coordination of support programmes
- Communication of product, market and corporate information.

Marketing support

Market development is key to the success of our strategy. Our marketing support programme includes an integrated range of marketing material including brochures, mailers, application information, presentations, sales manuals and product guides. To help you maximize sales opportunities we operate special pricing and promotional initiatives and we can provide customized support for your local marketing activities such as exhibitions, advertising, public relations or showroom displays. We also help you to make the most effective use of the marketing tools so that you can maximize the return from your marketing budgets.

Business development

We have considerable expertise in business development and we share this with you. For example, you can make use of our detailed market information to target the most important prospects and market sectors. You also benefit from the innovative range of products and services that ensure success in a changing marketplace. If you develop opportunities on larger accounts, you may also qualify for incentives by referring enquiries for larger prospects to us.

Technical support

You will receive direct technical support from the Dealer Support Group who have access to the nationwide resources of our Customer Service Division. We can also provide your engineers with technical training on new products and developments as well as installation and maintenance. We provide a wide range of technical publications and updates for you and your customers. Your customers can also make use of our nationwide service cover by taking one of our maintenance programmes. Through this programme, they can receive cover for up to 24 hours a day, 365 days a year from our National Service Centre.

Commercial support

The key to our mutual success is controlled profitable growth and you can make use of our financial strength and expertise to achieve that. We will help you plan sales and stock levels to meet growing customer demand and work with you to implement minimum stock levels that free cash to invest in growing your business. If necessary, we can provide you with financial support and other financial services through our own finance company so that you can concentrate on developing your business.

Becoming a dealer

In this brochure we have tried to give you an insight into our strategy and objectives. We believe our programmes lay the foundation for joint success and profitability in the market and we are committed to the growth and development of our dealer network. We would be delighted to talk to you in more detail about any aspect of the programme and we hope that you will consider becoming a dealer. If you would like to discuss the programme, please call us or write to the Dealer Sales Business Manager at the address shown on this publication. We will then send you a letter outlining the information we need to consider your application. This could be the beginning of a long, profitable association.

COMPETENCE SELF-ASSESSMENT

1 Describe the demand chain for your organization's products and services.
2 What criteria should you use for selecting suppliers?
3 How would you assess your suppliers' performance?
4 How would you increase your suppliers' involvement in your organization?
5 Describe how you could use information to improve supplier performance.
6 How could closer working relationships with distributors improve customer service?
7 What forms of support would help your retailers or distributors to operate more effectively? What impact would this have on customer service?
8 How can you improve control over your retail operations?
9 Describe the important aspects of your organization's relationships with its distributors.
10 Prepare a plan for a distributor support manual.

7 Making it easy to do business

If you make it easy for your customers to do business, you will build up a loyal customer base, but if you put barriers in their way, they will very quickly try the next supplier. This chapter looks at ways of improving the convenience of customer service, using a series of examples from different sectors.

HOW A TRAVEL AGENT EXPLOITS THE TELEPHONE

'The telephone is our lifeline and our staff are on the phone throughout the day, checking availability and prices, calling customers back and confirming reservations.' This independent travel agency group is typical of a number of retail organizations in the service sector who are making the most of the telephone services available from independent service providers.

Profile of the business

- Independent travel agent group with twelve branches
- Committed to quality customer service
- Planning data communication to enhance customer service
- Uses incoming call information to target marketing campaigns

- Considering 0800 freephone numbers to strengthen customer loyalty
- Utilizes outbound 0800 numbers to save staff time for customer service

'It's vital that we keep up to date with telecomms developments because they affect the way we do business, but we're too small to have a specialist on the staff. Our telecomms supplier fills that gap for us in a practical way. Our business is built on personal service and it's clear that they share the same attitude.'

The company is a group of independent travel agents with twelve branches around the south-east. The company concentrates on package holidays and business travel and sells the products of leading travel and tour operators. The company has identified a number of key business benefits in exploiting the telephone. According to the marketing manager:

'Quality customer service is vital in the travel business. If we can't give the customer the right answer quickly, our competitors will. The telephone is our lifeline and our staff are on the phone throughout the day, checking availability and prices, calling customers back and confirming reservations. We need a service we can rely on. The telephone has already proved itself on voice communications, we're now looking at the potential for data transmission. Most of our larger competitors are directly linked to computerised reservation systems. We have to compete with that, despite our size so we will be investing in a new system in the summer.'

The company is using reports on telephone responses to identify the location and demographics of the people who are interested in its services.

'The information helps us to make our marketing programmes better targeted. We are also discussing the potential for introducing freephone 0800 numbers for our

> regular customers, particularly the business travellers. I
> don't think we are ready for a freephone number for all
> callers, but I can see the loyalty benefits of giving it to our
> most important customers.'

The company is already using 0800 numbers for making outgoing calls as one of the branch managers explained:

> 'I was surprised when the Account Manager suggested this
> — I tend to associate 0800 numbers with customer service.
> But he had analysed our phone bills and he pointed out
> how many times we used a small group of numbers —
> mainly calls to certain suppliers or other branches. By
> using the 0800 number plus a short code, we can reduce
> dialling time. My staff are under a lot of pressure so
> anything that saves time is a bonus because it gives them
> more time for dealing with customers.'

Key benefits from the telephone

Enhanced customer service
Better market information
Easier access to travel
information
Increased customer
loyalty
Greater understanding of the
business contribution of
telecomms

Faster response to
enquiries
Improved targeting
Improved reliability
Improved call
productivity

SIMPLIFYING CUSTOMER CONTACT

When customers contact your organization for information, how easy is it for them to get through to the right contact? Here is how one organization is tackling the problem using a combination of freephone calling cards and customer numbers.

Freephone calling card

This is your personal calling card. You can use it to contact us with any queries or service requests. Whenever you want to contact us, all you have to do is dial the special 0800 number on the card followed by the code . . . You'll get straight through to a member of the Customer Service team and there will be no charge to you for the call. Don't forget to quote your customer number when you call.

If the Customer Service representative cannot deal directly with your call, he or she will make sure that you are put in touch with the appropriate specialist. We're sure you will find this a quick and convenient way to make calls and you may wish to make use of calling cards within your own organization to improve customer service and telephone productivity. You'll find brief information on the calling cards in your Customer Welcome Pack. If you would like more detail or if you would like to discuss applications in your own organization, contact the Customer Service team.

Customer number

This is your customer number. Please quote it whenever you contact us with any queries or service requests. The customer number helps us to have your account information and service records to hand when we talk to you. That way, we can deal with your call promptly and save you valuable time. Please keep this number handy. We have also included some other handy information you may wish to refer to quickly.

Your Customer Service Representative   NAME
Other Customer Service Representatives   NAMES . . . .
Customer Service telephone   NUMBER
Fax   NUMBER
Your personal calling card number   NUMBER

Single point of contact

Your customer number, plus the free 0800 number, provides you with a convenient, single point of contact for all services. A member of the Customer Service team will take the call and establish your exact requirements. If the Customer Service representative cannot deal with the enquiry, you will be transferred to an appropriate specialist. Please contact the Customer Service team initially with all your enquiries, including:

- Technical queries
- Service requests
- Customer service
- Order processing
- Invoice queries

- Helpline general queries
- Product information

A systematic approach like this helps to improve customer access and ensures that incoming callers are not taken 'round the houses' when they try to obtain information.

NATIONAL ENQUIRY CENTRES IMPROVE CUSTOMER CONVENIENCE

Simplifying customer access can improve customer convenience. By creating a central contact point for all customer enquiries, you can ensure that every incoming customer contact is handled efficiently. This is particularly appropriate for companies who have a number of separate locations or who are organized by product group. At the national enquiry centre all incoming calls are handled by a central reception centre and routed to the appropriate specialist. The customer does not have to waste time trying to track down the right contact. The centre should handle incoming calls for queries such as:

- Product information
- Technical information
- Service requests
- Literature
- Complaints
- Estimates and ordering
- Delivery
- Accounts

Many of these calls would be routed direct to the appropriate department, but an increasing number of companies are making the receptionist responsible for customer contact and incident management. For example, if a key customer makes a service request, the receptionist takes the basic details and arranges for a specialist to call the customer back within an agreed timescale. The receptionist may go further and maintain contact with the customer until the service problem has been resolved. The process is known as incident management and helps to reassure the customer that appropriate action is being taken.

Quality processes can be applied to call reception. For example, companies would be assessed on:

- Time to answer the call
- Time to respond to the customer
- Time to achieve a satisfactory result

The national enquiry centre is a valuable method of ensuring that the customer receives a consistent standard of quality service on every contact.

IMPROVING CUSTOMER TELEPHONE RESPONSE

If your business receives a high volume of incoming calls – sales, information or service queries, bookings or transaction processing – you need to ensure that those calls are answered quickly and efficiently. A quality response enhances customer service. Telecommunications technology now features user-friendly queuing techniques to ensure that calls are answered in sequence and no calls go unanswered. A system called Automatic Call Distribution (ACD) can be used to distribute incoming calls to a group of 'agents'. At any one time, some agents may be engaged while others are free to handle calls. The ACD system can be used to distribute the calls around the group:

- Incoming calls are queued and answered in order
- The system can be programmed to feed calls to waiting or specified agents automatically
- Calls are automatically routed to the longest waiting agent in a group
- If all agents in a group are busy, calls can overflow to a second group
- Calls can be routed to other groups after a preset ringing time.

A range of call processing options can be utilized to enhance call response even further:

- Integral call sequencing reduces the risk that callers will hang up by giving an informative message.
- Voicemail allows callers to leave messages for agents who are unavailable.
- Integrated Voice Response (IVR) order processing system answers callers automatically and takes details without agent intervention.
- Direct Dial Inward (DDI) allows callers to contact different members of staff directly via a personal telephone number, rather than through the switchboard. This can improve operational efficiency and offer a more personal customer service.
- Call Line Identification (CLI) is a service where your staff can identify the caller before answering the call. It improves customer service and ensures that calls are routed to the most appropriate staff.

■ CLI can be used in conjunction with Computer Telephony Interface (CTI) to provide individual customer information on a personal computer screen. This improves the efficiency of telephone order processing or the handling of enquiries and allows staff to deliver a more personal service.

These services are available on most digital telecommunications systems and your telecommunications supplier can provide further information.

VOICEMAIL MAKES IT EASIER FOR CUSTOMERS TO DEAL WITH YOU

Recent research from the telecommunications industry suggests that around 76% of calls are not completed at the first attempt. The extension is engaged, the contact is not there, or the caller got through to the wrong extension. It is frustrating for anyone who wants to place an order or make an enquiry, so how can you make it easier for customers to make contact? One solution would be to appoint more people to answer the phone, but that could be expensive and may not be cost-effective.

Callers may not want dialogue

Consider some further research findings – 50% of those calls were single-directional, the callers did not want to have a discussion, they just wanted to place an order or leave information. Is the solution to set up a central message centre? The research does little to encourage this approach. Of telephone messages taken by a third party 90% are believed to be inaccurate or incomplete in some way.

Give callers a choice

Voicemail is another possible solution. At its simplest, voicemail is the electronic equivalent of a personal mailbox. Callers can leave messages knowing that their contact will deal with them on their return. There is no problem in the accuracy of message handling and messages can be communicated to other people in the organization.

Voicemail can also be used as the basis of a sophisticated customer response system. For example, by keying certain digits, the caller can access information services, request literature, leave a private message, get through to an operator or initiate other actions.

Customer-focused response mechanism

By providing these options, a company can develop a customer-focused response mechanism that demonstrates high levels of customer care and convenience. Among the possible options are:

- 24-hour ordering systems that do not require staff presence
- Literature request service
- Dial-up price or delivery information service

Voicemail can be seen as an impersonal, machine-based system, but the customer service benefits are considerable.

IMPROVE CUSTOMER SERVICE WITH FREEPHONE NUMBERS

Freephone 0800 numbers are relatively new to the UK market and some organizations perceive them as expensive and suitable for larger companies. However, there are wide-ranging customer service applications and benefits and they are ideal for businesses of all sizes.

The importance of the telephone

- According to a recent report, 45% of companies have a dedicated telephone team in sales and customer service.
- By the year 2000, inbound calls are likely to exceed 400 million per annum, a fivefold increase in current levels.
- Research shows people are increasingly keen on buying by phone. In one survey, 70% of those interviewed claimed they found telephone ordering easy and convenient.

With the increasing emphasis on business by telephone, it is important to make telephone contact as simple as possible for customers. Freephone 0800 numbers are free to the customer, improving convenience and demonstrating customer care. They can be used to improve performance in many different customer service applications including:

- Reservation/enquiry lines – offering 0800 numbers to improve convenience for customers
- Product support – providing 0800 numbers for literature requests, product information, technical helplines
- Helplines – using 0800 numbers to encourage usage and build customer loyalty
- Customer loyalty – giving 0800 numbers to selected customers for free access to different types of service
- Major account support – providing 0800 numbers to major customers for ordering/enquiries/free access to switchboard/ dedicated helplines and support desks
- Telesales/mail order – using 0800 numbers for all enquiries/ orders
- Retail ordering – providing 0800 numbers for wholesalers/ retailers to order stock
- Literature requests – using different 0800 numbers for different publications or central brochure line
- Service requests – offering 0800 numbers to make it easier to place routine service requests
- Emergency/breakdown requests – providing 0800 numbers with 24-hour cover to minimize inconvenience in an emergency

The value of information on 0800 calls

Telecommunications suppliers can supply reports on incoming 0800 calls which provide valuable information on who is making them. This can be used to help identify new customer service opportunities. One company analysed its incoming 0800 calls over a week and realized that it was losing business by not opening on Saturdays when a large number of calls went unanswered. By introducing flexible working patterns, it was able to staff the telephones on Saturday and give employees a day off during the week when reports showed that the phones were quieter.

Analysis carried out by a mail order company showed that a large number of incoming 0800 calls were made during the evening, after the company had closed. They set up an evening telephone service to handle those calls and saw a significant increase in orders.

Using 0800 services

BT and Mercury are no longer exclusive suppliers of freephone services. There are many independent telecommunications providers and cable companies who can provide them. Set-up charges vary by supplier and, in some cases, are free. The other cost to you is the cost of the incoming calls.

OPTIONS FOR CUSTOMER RECEPTION

You can introduce the most sophisticated call-handling systems or set up computerized records that provide all the information you need to handle incoming calls efficiently, but what happens if the customer has a problem and there is no-one there to deal with the request? There are a number of options for handling customer enquiries outside normal working hours.

Provide 24-hour response

Customers usually have problems at the most inconvenient times. They may not need service immediately, but they feel more comfortable when they have reported a problem, discussed it with someone who knows what they are talking about and received reassurance that help will be on its way as quickly as possible. Out of hours, the service receptionist is likely to take details of the incident and make arrangements for all but the most urgent repairs the next working day. Twenty-four-hour cover can be provided in a number of ways:

- Setting up a shift system so that telephones are manned continuously
- Asking key personnel to take it in turns to handle emergency calls overnight; a call-diversion system can be used to route calls to their home number
- Provide customers with mobile phone or home phone numbers of key personnel
- Appoint an agency to provide an out-of-hours call-reception service.

Use 'postal reception'

This technique is used by car service companies or by companies that service small products. Typically a customer would have to wait until opening time just to hand over the keys or a product for repair. The customer may be late for work or suffer other inconvenience. With 'postal reception' the customer simply leaves the keys or the product in a secure area, such as a compound or mailbox. This means that the customer can leave the product whenever it is most convenient.

Offer 'call back' facilities

The customer may not be able to reach you during working hours or may want to talk to someone but cannot get through because the contact is busy. By setting up a telephone answering or fax facility, you can make it easy for your customers to leave a request for a 'call back'. Provided you reply promptly, customers will appreciate the high level of service and they will save money on their own phone calls.

Planning your customer reception strategy

Why do you need out-of-hours reception?
What type of enquiries will it handle?
What option will be appropriate?
What times will it be open?
Where will it be located?
What type of customer information will be needed?
What timescale will be needed for the full programme?
What are the major business benefits?

COMPETENCE SELF-ASSESSMENT

1 Describe how your organization could improve its use of the telephone.
2 How do customers contact your organization? How could you make it easier for them to make contact?
3 Prepare a plan for centralizing customer contact in your organization.
4 Is your organization making the most of telephone technology? Describe how you could call distribution technology to enhance service. Which departments would utilize it?
5 Prepare a plan for using voicemail to improve customer service.
6 How could freephone numbers be used to enhance customer service in your organization?
7 How do you currently handle customer reception and how could it be improved?
8 Is 24-hour service important to your business? Describe how you would implement it.
9 Prepare a plan for auditing your organization's use of the telephone.
10 Prepare an action plan to make it easier for your customers to do business.

8 Product development

Product development is one of the most important tasks your company faces. It ensures that your products always reflect customer needs and provides you with a source of long-term revenue and profitability. New products should not be developed in isolation, they should be based on comprehensive research into the needs of the market and, where possible, you should work closely with your customers to develop a product that provides mutual benefit. Existing products should not be overlooked. By enhancing those products or adding value to them with a range of after-market services, you can increase their customer appeal and improve market share.

THE PROCESS OF PRODUCT DEVELOPMENT

Product development is the process of focusing on customer needs to ensure that your product range continues to offer short- and long-term profit opportunities. There are five important stages in this process:

- Assess the life cycle position of your current product range.
- Look at your customers' own life cycle to identify product development opportunities.
- Operate a new product development programme.
- Operate a development strategy for existing products.
- Operate a service strategy to enhance products.

PRODUCT LIFE CYCLE

New products have a number of characteristics. They may be innovative in the marketplace which provides a strong competitive advantage, or they may be developed in response to an existing competitive product and therefore provide you with a means of market entry. They can involve high risk of failure and they require high levels of marketing support to establish a strong marketing position.

Growth products enjoy strong sales growth as market awareness and acceptance increases and the rate of growth is likely to be proportional to the investment of marketing effort. They may retain their innovative advantage for a period, but competitors are likely to respond. The emphasis may be on production, rather than customer service, to meet the growth in demand.

Mature products enjoy stable sales and there are likely to be smaller rates of growth or decline. There are likely to be established competitors with different levels of market share and the share of the market is likely to be proportional to the continued investment of marketing effort. There may be some product development to provide incremental gains or keep the product up to date.

Declining products have a number of characteristics. Sales decline as new consumer needs emerge. In some cases, competitors' product performance is superior, and your own product is no longer competitive. The share of the market is likely to decline as newer products gain consumer acceptance and there is unlikely to be any further development of existing products – the emphasis will be on new product development to regain competitive advantage. Marketing support will be reduced and reallocated to new or growth products.

Using the product life cycle

To make the most effective use of the product life cycle, you should take the following actions:

- Carry out research into customer requirements.
- Assess the comparative performance of competitive products.
- Assess customer attitudes to competitive products.
- Analyse your current planned product range to see whether it adequately meets current and future customer requirements.
- Modify your plans to meet any likely shortcomings.

CUSTOMER LIFE CYCLE

Another way to identify product development opportunities is to look at your customers' life cycle – how do they use your product and how can you help them make better use of it? These stages can be described as:

1   Consult
2   Design
3   Implement
4   Manage.

Consult

Customers will be deciding on their overall strategy for dealing with key business issues and you have an opportunity to influence the shape of future purchasing policy. You should be involved at this stage if you are facing high levels of competitive activity, particularly where competitors are trying to influence senior decision makers. You should also consider offering pre-sales and consultancy services as part of your overall package or solution.

Design

At this stage, your customer has decided the overall strategy and the purchasing department is consulting with individual departments to design specific solutions or incorporate individual requirements into the product specification. The customer is drawing up a detailed specification and you should consider offering further pre-sales and consultancy services, as well as specific design-based services.

Implement

Now, the new product is installed and customers concentrate their efforts on getting the new product up and running as quickly as possible with minimal disruption to day-to-day operations. You should consider offering support services such as project management and training.

Manage

The manage stage is the equivalent of normal operation. The product has been used successfully and your task is to ensure it continues to be used effectively and delivers business benefits. You should consider offering support services such as maintenance as part of your overall package or solution.

APPLYING THE CUSTOMER LIFE CYCLE

The customer life cycle can be applied to a number of business scenarios, particularly where customers are purchasing capital goods or are introducing new technology or new materials. There are a number of important considerations. Customers' needs change at each stage and their own support team may not have the skills or resources to handle all these tasks cost effectively. By identifying your customer's life cycle, you can develop a range of support services that will provide all the help and guidance that is needed, and you will be able to maintain high levels of contact with the customer throughout the ownership cycle. To make the most effective use of the customer life cycle approach, you need to build an understanding of your customer's business processes and get to know the skills and resources they have available. The life cycle gives you an opportunity to take over complete services on your customer's behalf or supplement their resources when they need help most.

NEW PRODUCT DEVELOPMENT PROGRAMMES

New products ensure that the company's product range continues to be focused on customer needs and remain competitive. There are four critical stages in the new product development process:

1   Planning product development programmes
2   Product research and customer consultation
3   Product development
4   Product launch.

PLANNING NEW PRODUCT DEVELOPMENT PROGRAMMES

There are many different approaches to planning new product development programmes:

- Making a corporate commitment to developing new products
- Analysing and responding to changes in the marketplace
- Utilizing the availability of new technology
- Working in partnership with customers to develop new products that meet their specific needs
- Identifying opportunities to enter new markets

Corporate commitment to new products

You decide that, as part of your overall marketing strategy, you will introduce a number of new products over a period of time. This approach can be driven by a number of factors. Market success depends on innovation, and this is particularly appropriate in high-technology markets. Research shows that customers perceive your product range as dated, while your competitors are perceived as innovative. Technology changes rapidly in your business, and it is important that your products reflect the latest technology.

Responding to changes in the marketplace

You may not take the initiative on new product development, but simply respond to initiatives by competitors. This approach can be driven by a number of factors. Your competitors are gaining market share with new products. Your own products are seen as outdated. New technology developed by competitors is now available to your company. Research shows that your customers prefer competitive products.

Utilizing the availability of new technology

New products can be influenced by the availability of new technology. However, this approach should be used with caution. There may not be a market for the product or product performance may exceed market requirements. The market may be cautious about the risk in using new technology. This approach can be driven by a number of factors:

- You can obtain an exclusive license to new technology, giving you an immediate competitive advantage.
- The new technology will enable you to enhance the performance of existing products and gain a competitive advantage.
- The new technology may enable you to meet market requirements that had previously been unobtainable.

Working in partnership with customers

Product development can be a joint initiative where you work closely with specific customers to develop products that meet their specific needs. This approach can be driven by a number of factors. Your customer has developed partnership sourcing to take advantage of your technology. Your customer has technical skills that complement your own and a joint project can produce more effective results. Your customer has technology that will prove valuable to your own product development programme and there is an opportunity for mutual benefit. You want to strengthen relationships with key customers by working in partnership on joint development projects.

KEY MANAGEMENT ACTIONS TO IMPLEMENT NEW PRODUCT DEVELOPMENT PROGRAMMES

New product development does not happen by accident. It is a process that must be planned and supported with commitment, resources and funding. There are a number of essential management actions:

- Make a commitment at board level to new product development.
- Allocate sufficient resources and funding to new product development.
- Communicate the importance of new product development to all employees.
- Provide adequate resources to launch new products effectively.

There are a number of stages in the product development process:

- Setting programme objectives
- Establishing a new product development team
- Identifying the development route
- Setting schedules
- Pilot programmes
- Customer consultation.

Programme objectives

A product development programme should have specific objectives. The programme should not operate in a vacuum because its results may not be commercially viable:

- The programme objectives should reflect the findings of product and market research.
- Product development objectives should be in line with corporate objectives.
- Programme objectives should be specific, for example improve product performance by $x\%$, develop a new product to meet the following specification.

Product development teams

New product development is not an activity that is carried out by a research and development unit. The process should involve many different people, including:

- Research and development staff to carry out the detailed work
- Product managers to develop the programme requirements
- Marketing managers to ensure that the product meets customer requirements

- Manufacturing managers to ensure that the product can be manufactured cost-effectively
- Customer representatives if the programme is a joint development.

Product development routes

There are a number of ways to approach new product development:

- Carrying out fundamental research and development work to create a completely new product
- Modifying existing products to provide higher performance or to meet different operating requirements
- Developing new products based on competitive specifications
- Adding new features to existing products
- Tailoring existing products to meet the requirements of specific customers

Setting schedules

The speed of new product development programmes can be a vital factor in ensuring their success. The programme schedule should include a number of intermediate stages:

- A pilot programme to test the new products and assess customer reaction
- Phase review meetings to assess the continuing viability of the programme. If a programme does not research well or meet its objectives, it may need to be abandoned
- Customer consultation to ensure initial acceptance of the programme

Pilot programmes

A pilot programme can be valuable in assessing the potential success of the programme. It can be used to evaluate product performance, customer acceptance, weight of launch material required or distribution requirements. Pilot programmes can take a number of forms:

- Testing the product with a small number of customers who agree to provide feedback
- Launching the product in a specific region as a prelude to a full launch

■ Handling a test launch with a targeted direct marketing programme which simulates a number of the launch conditions

Customer consultation

Consulting customers about new product developments can have a number of important benefits. Customers are involved in the development process and are aware of your future developments. Customer feedback can form a valuable input to the development process and customers can incorporate the new developments in their own product development programmes.

The process of consultation can take a number of forms:

■ Communicating new developments to customers through product releases
■ Arranging pilot trials with selected customers
■ Setting up user groups to assess new products.

DEVELOPING EXISTING PRODUCTS

New product development is not the only option for improving product performance. Existing products should also go through a continuous process of review and development to ensure that they remain focused on changing customer needs. There are a number of different approaches to product development:

■ Responding to competitive product actions
■ Enhancing the product with additional features and benefits
■ Using value engineering to improve overall product performance for the customer
■ Implementing a product range strategy
■ Introducing 'own label' products
■ Buying in products or services from third parties

Responding to competitive actions

This strategy is important if you are in a competitive marketplace. By matching competitive actions you can ensure that you retain market share, but the strategy could result in a defensive attitude that does not take your company forward.

Enhance the product with additional features and benefits

This strategy is suitable for developing existing products in a growth or mature phase. The strategy can be based on an assessment of customer needs or a policy of matching competitive actions. It can take a number of forms:

- Improving performance or enhancing the product to provide a competitive edge
- Improving performance to reflect customer requirements
- Enhancing the product while maintaining the same price

Example
A furniture company which markets kitchen units for home assembly introduces three actions to enhance the product. The company now offers a choice of eight finishes, compared with six for its nearest rivals. In line with research findings, the company introduces rigid drawer construction. Finally, the company introduces a free estimating and planning service, while retaining prices at the previous year's level.

Using value engineering to improve overall product performance for the customer

Value engineering is the process of evaluating all the customer's costs of owning a product to see if some of those costs can be reduced. The strategy is important in markets where there is little difference between products and the market is very competitive. The strategy requires the following actions:

- Analyse the way the customer uses the product.
- Assess the customer's costs in after-sales activities such as assembling, fitting, distributing or maintaining the final product.
- Identify opportunities to reduce any of those customer costs by modifying your product or service.
- Review your proposals with the customer to ensure that they understand the benefits.

Example
A bearing manufacturer supplying transmission bearings worked closely with an equipment manufacturer to

rationalize the design of a new product through value engineering. By substituting a transmission bearing with integral housing, sealing and lubrication facility for a series of separate components, the manufacturer was able to reduce machining and assembly costs. The bearing supplier was able to put considerable distance between his added-value engineering solution and a standard component, and overcome price comparisons. The company was also able to build closer working relationships with the design department and to build future modifications and product developments into the customer's future plans.

Implementing a product range strategy

In this strategy you use the reputation and success of your existing products to sell more products through the same sales channels. The strategy has a number of important features:

- Products added to an existing range offer customers a greater choice.
- The additional products may make the range more attractive to prospects.
- The new products benefit from the marketing support given to existing products in the range.
- A range strategy provides an opportunity to increase the value of sales per customer without a proportional increase in marketing costs.
- The new products should be based on research into customer needs.
- Range extension is an important element of a relationship marketing programme.

Example

A motoring organization which offers roadside rescue services recognizes the benefits of its membership base. It introduces a range of motoring-related services such as maps, travel information and insurance services to increase the overall value of customer purchases. The range of basic motoring rescue services is also extended to give members a greater choice. Depending on their motoring habits, members can select a simple rescue service, a recovery service that gets them to their destination or a comprehensive service that provides them with a choice of recovery services wherever they break down. Each of the range extensions builds on the existing reputation and helps to increase customer loyalty.

Introducing 'own-label' products

A company that markets products under its own name can also increase sales by developing modified products for sale by other organizations under their names. The strategy has a number of possible approaches:

- Repackaging standard products in the own-label identity
- Modifying the product to meet the other manufacturer's specifications
- Developing a product specifically for the other manufacturer.

Example

A construction equipment manufacturer supporting its customers through a network of distributors develops a range of own-label replacement parts which carry its own branding. The products are sourced from specialist manufacturers, but are manufactured to the company's specification and quality standards. The parts range enables the manufacturer to strengthen its relationship with customers and provides incremental business for the components manufacturers.

Buying in products or services from third parties

This strategy, like the own-label strategy, allows companies to enhance their own product performance without investing in their own product development. There are a number of possible approaches:

- Subcontract product development to an outside organization
- Buy existing products that complement or extend a range
- Buy a complete product range from a third party

■ Work in partnership with a third party to jointly develop a new product or service.

TAKING THE RISK OUT OF NEW PRODUCTS

The words 'new technology' or 'complete solution' can be intimidating to customers and create resistance to the successful launch of new products.

A mobile communications company carried out a survey among customers and prospects to assess attitudes towards new communications technology. The survey highlighted a concern that new technology involved high levels of risk and change, and could cause disruption to the business while it was integrated with existing day-to-day working practices. The survey also indicated that potential customers felt unsure about evaluating the business benefits of new technology and feared that they would make a wrong choice because of the 'mystique' surrounding the product.

The company decided to demystify its products and offer them as 'packaged' solutions which could be bought off the shelf and used immediately. This removed the risk of long-running development and implementation programmes feared by some customers and ensured that they would enjoy an easy entry into new technology. The company emphasized that it also offered tailored products to customers with more complex requirements, but it felt that it was more important to broaden the market by making entry-level technology more accessible.

The packaged approach has also been used successfully in the computer software market and by subscription products such as car rescue services. The approach not only reduces risks, it also improves customer service.

GETTING THE NEW PRODUCT MESSAGE ACROSS

Launching a new product is a major event which can have significant consequences for a company's future success and profitability. To ensure the success of the launch, you have to convince a number of different groups to give their commitment to the product.

Business presentations form an important part of the process of building commitment, and these can take a number of forms:

1 Strategic presentation to the executive team to ensure that the new product development and launch is fully supported at every stage
2 Management team presentation on key activities to ensure that everyone understands their role in the programme
3 Salesforce briefing to build commitment and understanding of the new product

4   National dealer launch to achieve distribution and commitment to sales
5   Customer presentation to introduce the product to key accounts and support the salesforce
6   Press launch to raise media interest and support the communications process

To help you develop your own scripts for the different types of presentation, the following are some examples of key messages for each audience.

Executive team presentation

A new product development programme is unlikely to succeed if it does not have the full support of top management. The programme needs funds and resources, as well as the support of top management to push through change. To gain the right level of commitment, the new product is positioned as an integral part of the company's future strategy.

> 'As you know, volume and profit in our traditional markets is shrinking as new competitors enter and the pace of technological change increases. Our product range is perceived as old-fashioned and research shows that our rating as an innovative supplier is declining. To correct that situation, we need to develop a new range of high-performance products which will re-establish our position as market leader.'

This presentation sets out the requirements for the programme in broad terms and demonstrates its importance to the company's future.

Management team presentation

A product launch involves a number important steps to ensure success, so it is essential that the key responsibilities are communicated. A complex launch involves good working relationships between research, marketing, manufacturing and sales departments so that each department can make an effective timely contribution to the process.

> The timescale for launching the new product is extremely tight and success will depend on integration of all the key activities. We aim to set up a project team which covers all

> the main departmental functions. We will be using
> simultaneous engineering to develop the product in the
> timescale available, and we believe this degree of coopera-
> tion can be applied to other functions.'

This outlines the main support programme which the marketing department
will be operating. It provides them with information on the main programme
requirements and ensures that they have sufficient time to plan their
strategy.

Salesforce briefing

Salesforce commitment is crucial to the success of the launch. Unless the
salesforce put the right amount of effort into the launch, it will not reach its
launch targets and could lose momentum. But to launch the new product
effectively, the salesforce must believe in it, they must be convinced that it will
benefit their customers.

> 'Research shows that there is pent-up demand for a
> technically advanced product; we have designed our new
> product range to meet and exceed the requirements
> shown in the research programme and we believe
> prospects will be extremely receptive to this initiative. To
> help you generate interest in the marketplace, we will be
> running a press information programme with feature
> articles on the technical performance of the new product
> range. We will also make available a number of demonstra-
> tion models which can be offered to important customers
> for a trial period. We believe that this will generate high
> levels of interest in the marketplace and make your task
> more manageable.'

The salesforce need to be reassured that they are selling a product the market
wants. Research and a communications programme which provides direct
feedback on customer attitudes can help to build that confidence. The salesforce
also need a great deal of information on the product. Provided the salesforce has
the right level of product knowledge, it should be able to sell the new product
with confidence. It may, however, take more than confidence and commitment
to achieve sales targets.

'To reward members of the salesforce who exceed their launch targets, we will be operating a structured incentive programme which includes a number of different elements. Points will be awarded for key account demonstrations, sales and after-market sales of service contracts. We will also be awarding points for levels of product knowledge to ensure that you have the skills to present the product effectively.'

The incentive programme is a well-proven method for motivating the salesforce, but here it is structured to encourage the salesforce to acquire a high level of product knowledge and develop after-market sales as a means of retaining customer loyalty after the initial launch.

National dealer launch

Dealers can be the essential link between customers and manufacturers. Although they are involved in the direct sales process, they may handle smaller accounts rather than the national accounts which would be handled directly by the company salesforce. The distributor's contribution to the success of a product launch is significant. They represent the company to a large number of customers and they must be able to demonstrate the same level of product knowledge and market awareness as the company salesforce.

'We are introducing a new range of high-performance products which will enable you to compete effectively in a strong growth market. The products are designed to reflect the requirements of the marketplace and we have already had positive feedback on a number of prototypes which have been on trial at key customer sites. Research shows that the new product range will appeal to your own customer profile and will therefore fit well into your own portfolio. We believe that they will enhance our joint reputation for innovative products and will make a major contribution to our long-term business success.'

The product is positioned as a valuable means of building distributor business with the after-market, and with new prospects. Distributors are not just handling another product, they are achieving valuable business benefits.

Customer presentation

If the product is high value, there may be opportunities to make presentations direct to the customer's own management team. With a complex technical product, the presentation would be aimed at a number of different members of the team. The design team would be the important target for a technical presentation.

'The new range sets new standards of performance in the market and will enable you to reach all your design targets. You will be able to improve the speed and performance of your operations and that will help you develop new business opportunities. To help you make full use of the new product range, we will be running a series of seminars and workshops on your premises, and we will be issuing a comprehensive designers' guide.'

The success of the product launch can be affected by the current perception of the supplier. If research shows that the company's product range is perceived as old-fashioned, the presentation will have to work hard to reposition the company in the minds of corporate decision makers.

Press launch

Press information can help to support the sales drive by raising awareness and interest in the new product. A press launch can be exaggerated by hype but, used properly, it can help to reinforce the direct sales effort.

'The new product range has been designed to fill an important gap in the market by providing a high-performance product at a realistic price. The product is the result of an extensive research and development programme and meets customer specifications identified in a wide-ranging customer survey. The product will be supported by introductory consultancy and project management services and will help customers to achieve new standards of performance. Full performance information is provided in your press pack and, if you have any questions, we can put you in touch with specialists.'

This presentation is low-key, providing information and not overselling the product. The press respond to information, rather than hype and are willing to provide good coverage if the product represents genuine benefits, rather than exaggerated claims.

COMPETENCE SELF-ASSESSMENT

1 How do your organization's products fit into the product life cycle?
2 Describe the life cycle position of three of your customers.
3 Prepare a new product development plan for your organization.
4 Describe the new product development team and list their contribution.
5 Prepare a plan for enhancing your existing product range.
6 How would you use value engineering techniques to improve your existing products?
7 Describe a new technology which could be adopted by your organization.
8 Prepare an action plan for a new product launch.
9 Describe how you would inform key people in the organization about new product development.
10 Describe the customer benefits of a new high-technology product developed by your organization.

9 Adding value with services

Adding value to a product or service helps to differentiate products from the competition and improves standards of customer service. By analysing the products and services in your range you can add value and improve customers' perception of your organization. The following are some examples:

- Business services that free customer staff to do more important tasks or help managers perform their jobs better. Training, for example, can help a company make more of the products it buys by ensuring that staff can make effective use of them.
- Accessories can make a consumer product such as a camera more attractive.
- Convenience services added to a basic service enhance it – insurance companies, for example, might add a helpline or list of approved repairers to help their customers recover more quickly from an accident.

This chapter provides guidelines on adding value to your products and services.

PRODUCT/SERVICE PACKAGES

To add value to products and to increase customer loyalty, companies are putting together 'bundles' of products and services that reflect customer needs. Table 9.1 shows examples of different approaches to bundling and unbundling.

Table 9.1

Process	Examples
Adding in services	Package holidays including flight, hotel, transport
	Out-of-town retail sites offering greater convenience of parking and distribution
Leaving out services	'Fastfit' car repair centres leave out non-essential services
	Direct banking leaves out premises
	Direct insurance leaves out intermediaries
Changing infrastructure	Electronic newspapers
	Home shopping
Added value	Home delivery of fast food
	Personal breakdown/recovery/onward transport
	Support and advice through helplines
	Personal computers for home entertainment
Changing distribution channels	Direct/sales bypassing retailers
	Electronic delivery such as ATMs replacing bank counter service.

The exercise below will help you and your staff understand the concept of 'added value' and enable you to add value to their own products and services. Listed below are twenty products and services. List beside each as many added-value services as you think are appropriate.

Product/service

1 Car repairs
2 Household insurance
3 Magazine subscription
4 Sports club membership
5 Management consultancy
6 Computer maintenance
7 Airline reservation

8 Mobile telephone network
9 Office stationery supplier
10 Plumber
11 Coach operator
12 Training consultancy
13 Business bank
14 Radio station
15 Garden centre
16 Car hire company
17 TV rental company
18 Petrol station
19 Credit card issuer
20 Architect

ENHANCING YOUR CUSTOMERS' SKILLS

How can you make it easier for your customers to do business with you? By simplifying ordering and purchase administration through added-value services, you can increase customer convenience and build customer loyalty. The following simple example based on a components supplier shows how information and training can contribute.

Product and technical support

- Provide microfiche terminal plus microfiches on products.
- Provide access to members of the parts team for advice and guidance.
- Offer technical support via telephone with site visits if needed.
- Ensure that product information is updated regularly.
- Provide helpline support.
- Offer access to the manufacturer's technical support resources.
- Recommend monthly meeting to review technical issues.

Training for customer staff

- Arrange exchange visits.
- Provide training on the identification of parts.
- Provide training on using microfiche information.
- Offer opportunities for customer staff to train at manufacturer's training centre.
- Ensure a parts specialist is available to resolve parts-identification problems.

BUSINESS SUPPORT

- Provide information on parts purchasing patterns.
- Help customers to identify purchasing trends
- Help customers to rationalize parts operations to improve overall performance.
- Supply management information in a form to suit customers' reporting systems.
- Offer the option of your own parts specialist on the customer site to control parts acquisition, freeing up their staff and ensuring an even faster response.

MENU PRICING

Menu pricing can improve customer satisfaction by offering customers a degree of choice when they are faced with bills for large purchases. Can you break down the products or services you offer into different modules? Can you offer specific customer groups different levels of the same service? Examples might include:

- Car servicing – complete service or oil and filter change
- Maintenance contracts – gold service or bronze service
- Club membership – full membership, associate membership

The following are some examples of products that have been broken down into menu options:

Car servicing
Full service   Interim service
Oil and filter change   Brake/steering check
Engine tune-up   Electrical check

Domestic appliance cover
Extended warranty – 2 years   Extended warranty – 5 years

Vehicle rescue services
Roadside assistance   Recovery to home or garage
Transportation to destination   Home assistance
European recovery/rescue   Complete service

Disaster recovery service
Alternative accommodation   Custom-designed replacement offices
Contingency planning services   Temporary accommodation

The menu approach allows you to offer the customer a level of service that is appropriate to their needs and affordable. It also helps you to make better use of your resources and skills and provides the customer with choice and convenience.

IMPROVING THE VALUE OF RESCUE SERVICES

A company providing car accident recovery services increased its business with fleet operators and insurance companies by concentrating on customer service.

The company provides a complete accident management service to fleet operators, insurance companies who wish to increase the benefits offered to their customers, companies who want to provide managers or staff with a 'car care' service and dealerships who want to offer car buyers added-value service.

Through research and focus groups, insurance companies and fleet operators told the company that they wanted three things from an accident management service:

1   Minimum inconvenience for their drivers
2   Rapid quality repair service, regardless of where the accident takes place
3   Real value for money

When the company developed its service, the following were the key considerations:

■   *Driver care is the priority*   One phone call from anywhere in the country puts the service into action. A central incident controller will ensure that one of the company's local teams provides the driver with a replacement car or makes other arrangements to suit the driver. Whatever happens, inconvenience is minimal and driver satisfaction is increased.
■   *Ensuring consistent standards of repair*   The company wanted to ensure that standards of repair were consistent throughout the country. Rather than sub-contract the work, they established their own nationwide network of body-shops so that they had total control over the repair process. Each of the sites was accredited to BS 5750 so that they could guarantee the same quality standards wherever the repair is carried out.
■   *Ensuring value for money*   The company knew that margins were tight in the insurance business, so they made a significant investment in training and equipment throughout the network so that they can complete repairs quickly at really competitive prices.

HOW THE SERVICE OPERATES

The service has a number of key elements:

- One point of contact for drivers, 24 hours a day. One number – freecall 0500 123999 – puts the driver in touch with the incident control room. Support is coordinated from that point on by trained staff using the latest communications technology.
- A rapid nationwide response from a nationwide network of bodyshops. Wherever the accident occurs, the company has its own local specialists to take care of the driver and the car, quickly and with the minimum of fuss.
- An emphasis on driver care, with a replacement vehicle at the site of the accident, or a choice of onward transport or accommodation if the driver is unable to continue driving.
- The highest standards of car care. Through their own bodyshops, the company provides consistent quality repair standards to maintain manufacturers' warranty requirements.
- Efficient control and administration. The company keeps customers fully informed on progress during the repair process.
- Cost-effective solution. The company offers competitive prices to minimize customers' repair and operating costs, and they also reduce the customer's own management involvement by controlling every aspect of the recovery and repair process on their behalf.

This is a unique service, focused on customer needs and one that will make a major contribution to customer's operating efficiency.

HOW THE COMPANY CONTROLS LOCAL STANDARDS

The quality of service would suffer if the local bodyshop was not able to deliver the correct standard of service. An important part of their task is to ensure that customers receive the same standards of service wherever they happen to break down. The company has strategically located bodyshops throughout the country. Regardless of where the accident occurs, a local outlet is close, usually just a short distance away from most major routes.

Consistent quality nationwide

When the company researched customer needs they found that customers were concerned at varying standards of repair from different bodyshops. Companies who simply manage accidents and place the repairs with independent bodyshops have only a limited degree of control over standards of work and cannot guarantee consistency. The company decided from the outset that it would own its bodyshops and each site is accredited to BS 5750, as well as conforming to group standards.

Attention to detail

The company concentrated on the atmosphere and the working environment. Staff took a great deal of pride in their work and they liked to show it. Customers found polished floors and fresh paintwork – not the sort of thing they would expect in a bodyshop, but it was indicative of their attention to detail.

The latest equipment

The company invested in the latest equipment and technology to speed up repairs, and they used quality refinishing systems with computerized paint mixing to ensure the highest standards of refinishing.

Caring for the environment

All the bodyshops are approved by local authorities under the Environmental Protection Act. The company operates a programme of responsible care in handling paints and waste materials and they are using materials that are environmentally friendly and that minimize emission levels.

Comprehensive training

Staff attend specialist repair or refinishing courses to ensure that they are familiar with the latest techniques. The company also puts a great deal of emphasis on customer care training, so that staff are aware of the importance of looking after the customer, as well as the car.

Capacity

Each of the bodyshops has the capacity to handle high volumes of repairs and local bodyshops also pool their resources so that really urgent repairs can be carried out on another site if necessary. They use the latest computerized bodyshop control systems to optimize workload and ensure the fastest possible turnround for customers' vehicles.

Approvals

All the bodyshops in the group are approved by major insurance companies and many of them are approved by leading manufacturers so that they can ensure that repairs meet manufacturers' warranty requirements.

CARING FOR DRIVERS

Driver care is the company's number one priority. They understand the problems and distress accidents can cause and their aim is to minimize inconvenience to the driver. They give drivers an information pack that tells them all about the service and gives detailed instructions on what to do in the event of an accident.

One freephone number, 24 hours a day

Drivers don't have the problems of trying to locate a bodyshop or recovery service, find change for the phone or worry about what will happen next. One call to the company's freephone help desk puts them in touch with an incident controller who will coordinate all rescue and recovery activities. All drivers have to do is quote their membership number and give details of their location and the company takes care of the rest.

Support throughout the incident

The staff at the control centre maintain contact throughout an incident to ensure that everything is coordinated. They use the latest telephone technology to respond rapidly to enquiries and they have access to local computers so that they can monitor progress on recovery and repair. Most important, the staff are trained to provide support and guidance to drivers who may be distressed after an accident.

A replacement car to the accident site

There are no problems about alternative transport. The company takes a car to the driver who is free to continue the journey immediately. This puts the driver's mind at rest and puts them back in control straight away. The company takes care of the damaged car while the driver has use of the replacement car until their own vehicle is returned to them.

Transport or accommodation options

Drivers may prefer to use other forms of transport or to stay overnight in a hotel if they are not able to drive straight away. The company will make all the necessary arrangements on their behalf and cover their costs up to agreed limits. Again, they will not have the problem of trying to make arrangements when they may be distressed and when they do not have funds to cover unexpected costs.

Increased driver satisfaction

The company believes that, by offering this high level of driver support, the customer will be seen as a caring organization and this can increase levels of employee or customer loyalty.

MANAGING THE REPAIR PROCESS

Accident management can be a time-consuming process, so the company takes care of every aspect for the customer, leaving them free to concentrate on more important management tasks.

Controlling costs

The company provides fully detailed, itemized estimates and they ensure that the car is inspected by a qualified engineer. All costs are strictly controlled through standard workshop times and they ensure that the vehicle is back on the road in the shortest possible time.

Reporting procedures

The company provides comprehensive reports of the repair costs of all a customer's vehicles on a monthly, quarterly or annual basis. They can also provide management information in a form that is suitable for the customer's own corporate reporting systems.

A CUSTOMER-DRIVEN QUALITY SERVICE

This service is driven by customer needs at every stage. The company has paid considerable attention to detail and control to ensure that every customer receives a consistent standard of service, wherever they are.

WINNING A MAJOR CONTRACT ON SERVICE

A components supplier pitched for a contract with a national chain of accident repair specialists. The accident repair company stressed that it would make its decision not on price, but on the quality of service. Service would be important because it aimed to deliver the highest standards of customer service. Any problems in components supply would have an impact on its customer service performance. Table 9.2 shows the key elements of the components supplier's offer.

SERVICE PACKAGES – AN EFFECTIVE WAY TO STRENGTHEN CUSTOMER RELATIONSHIPS

Customer services such as consultancy, planning, installation, training and maintenance are provided by many companies free as part of an overall package. However, high-value services can offer both you and your customers important strategic benefits and they should be included as an integral element of a customer service programme.

Table 9.2

Offer	Customer benefit
7-day-a-week service with agreed levels of cover	Confidence that delivery will be available whenever it is needed
Direct telephone line	Convenience – easier access to supplier
Dedicated parts team with named contacts	The supplier's staff understand the customer's business. Customer has an immediate point of contact
Scheduled and emergency deliveries in line with your requirements	Flexibility and reliability. The customer is not limited to a standard service
Stock cover of more than 11 000 lines	Efficiency. The stock levels are sufficient to meet the majority of requirements immediately. The customer is unlikely to be let down
Rapid sourcing of non-stock parts	Reliability. The customer can make alternative plans confident that any parts problems will be resolved quickly
Quality processes covering all parts operations	Confidence that the repair work will be right first time
Simple ordering procedures	Convenience and a reduction in administrative effort for the customer
Comprehensive product information/technical support and advice	Improves the performance of the customers' own staff
Management information on parts supply	Improves the customer's procurement operations with the potential to identify additional improvements
Customer satisfaction monitoring and escalation processes	Confidence that the supplier is committed to high standards of customer service

Maintaining account control

Look at your customers' buying cycle. How frequently do they make purchases – monthly, annually, every three years, every five years? The longer the purchase cycle, the more difficult it is to retain account control. Other companies can be talking to your customers, users may be experiencing problems that you are not aware of, and the decision-making team may be changing in ways that you cannot influence. Loss of contact could mean loss of control.

In the consumer sector, car manufacturers realized that the period between new car sales is the most critical element of customer relations. With customers buying new cars every two to three years on average, sales control is minimal. Manufacturers have therefore focused their efforts on building an effective after-sales operation based on the fact that parts and service operations generate five times the number of customer contacts as new car sales.

The manufacturers realized that they had been losing both repair and scheduled maintenance work to 'fast-fit' operations. This meant a loss of revenue to their dealerships, but also denied them the opportunity to maintain customer satisfaction between car purchases.

The same principle can be applied to markets where new product sales have similar purchase lead times of several years. Computer manufacturers had been losing maintenance business to independent service companies. They also found that the customers' information systems strategy and choice of systems was being driven not by the manufacturers but by management consultancies.

When management consultancies moved into other areas of information systems service such as application development and managed service and when independent service companies expanded their activities the computer manufacturers lost even more account control. Although service companies and management consultancies were not the manufacturers' direct competitors, they were enjoying high levels of contact with key decision makers at senior and middle management level, and this influenced future business opportunities.

By introducing a broad range of services, the manufacturers would be able to build high levels of contact with decision makers throughout the customer organization.

Improving loyalty and contact

Customer contact is one of the most important benefits of a service programme. If we take the example of the computer manufacturer, we can identify a number of stages where customer service can be used to increase the frequency and quality of customer contact:

- *Pre-sales consultancy* – helping the customer develop a strategy in line with corporate objectives. This brings the company into contact with the senior executive team and provides valuable information on the customer's future business plans.
- *Planning* – turning the strategy into a practical solution. This provides contact opportunities at senior executive and operational levels.
- *Implementation services* – helping the customer to install and introduce a new product without recruiting specialist staff or overloading their own support staff. This helps to ensure that the customer's product is implemented effectively, increasing customer satisfaction and loyalty.
- *Training services* – providing the customer with skills development and building useful contact with departmental managers and users.

■ *Managed services* – which cover a wide range of maintenance services. This provides the supplier with one of the best opportunities for continuous contact with the customer and gives the supplier a valuable insight into the customer's changing product needs.

Identifying service opportunities

One of the most effective ways to identify service opportunities is to look at the problems your customers face by analysing a series of business scenarios. Some examples show how the process works.

Customer needs
Objective advice
Defining problems
Adapt quickly to change
Short-term resources
Develop new skills
Continued service operation

Your customers need to ensure that they have devised the right strategy to meet their business objectives. They need objective advice and guidance to improve the quality of their own decision making. You could meet those requirements by offering consultancy services.

Your customers have identified certain activities which are crucial to their business success. They need help in defining the problems and planning the most appropriate course of action. Consultancy will also be relevant here.

Your customers need to adapt quickly to changing market conditions or competitive threats, but they do not have the resources or skills to succeed. You can offer your customers your skills and resources on a project basis so that they can overcome short- and long-term requirements.

Your customers need to develop new user and management skills so that they can get the best return from the products and services they have bought from you. You can offer your customers training services.

Your customers need to ensure that their products are continually operational and providing the business benefits for which they were designed. By offering your customers maintenance services or managing their equipment for them, you can ensure that their products are kept in the best possible condition.

These business scenarios help you to identify opportunities for offering services to your customers. Customers may provide many of these services from their own resources, but it is possible to get further involved through the growth in outsourcing.

Outsourcing opportunities

Outsourcing is a growing trend in companies seeking to concentrate on their core business, rather than attempting to do everything themselves. By using outside specialists to handle activities such as maintenance, systems management, distribution, fleet management and customer support, companies can make better use of their own resources and benefit from a quality, cost-effective service from suppliers who specialize in the activity. Outsourcing provides an opportunity to build closer relations with your key account customers by offering them vital services.

Service standards

Superior service standards can differentiate a supplier, so it is important that you position your company as a quality service supplier. Your customers will assess your performance according to a number of factors:

- Adherence to an independent quality standard such as BS 5750
- Your service response mechanism – how quickly and easily can customers contact you when they have a query or a problem?
- Your service infrastructure – spares level, service network, location and number of service specialists, investment in service tools
- Your capability for managed service – training, management resources, administrative support and ability to coordinate other specialists
- Your service performance – response times, success rate, your measurement of customer satisfaction and your escalation procedures for problems that cannot be resolved

If you are serious about using customer services to improve account control, you need to ensure that you can provide a specialist quality service that enhances your corporate reputation. The importance of customer services has led many suppliers to reposition themselves as 'total solutions' companies providing not just products but all the supporting services that will enable their customers to achieve full business benefit from their investment in the product.

COMPETENCE SELF-ASSESSMENT

1　Describe a range of product/service packages suitable for your organization.
2　Which services could you 'leave out' without reducing the quality of customer service?
3　Describe the product and technical services offered by your organization.
4　Give examples of menu pricing suitable for your organization.
5　What are the key customer service considerations for your organization's products?
6　How can you ensure consistent standards of service across all your operations?
7　Describe the customer benefits of your service operations.
8　Describe the ownership cycle for your organization's products.
9　Which added-value services could be offered at different stages of the ownership cycle?
10　Does outsourcing provide you with opportunities to add value to the customer relationship?

10 Improving quality

Managing quality is an integral part of the process of meeting your customers' needs. The subject of quality is a broad one and detailed discussion lies outside the scope of this book. If you wish to review the subject in more detail, please see *Managing Quality* (Wilson, Cairns, McBride and Bell, Butterworth-Heinemann, 1994). However, quality depends on the attitude of people as much as systems, and this chapter therefore provides guidelines on actions which can help you to build an environment for continuous improvement.

CUSTOMER FOCUS THROUGH SELF-ASSESSMENT

Quality and self-assessment are vital to any company's success. The aim is to identify best practice for a range of customer-facing jobs and try to beat it. The secret is continuous improvement – making lots of small changes work, rather than trying to force through one major change. Through quality and self-assessment, companies can achieve their our objective of increasing customer satisfaction. This section explains how one company approached self-assessment.

Why self-assessment is important

- Quality is critical to both short- and long-term success.

- Self-assessment enables effective measurement and monitoring of performance and provides a focus for quality initiatives among all employees.
- In many organizations, customer satisfaction and profitability have improved in parallel with performance against self-assessment criteria.

The role of quality

Quality is integral to a long-term business strategy. The company is committed to the highest standards of quality and customer service. They want to delight all their customers by exceeding their expectations time after time, and they aim to be recognized as the number one for customer satisfaction. In short, they want to be a company that customers are proud to do business with.

According to the quality manager:

'Quality is about listening to our customers and delivering more than they expect. It's about paying attention to the smallest details and "getting it right first time, every time". Most important, quality is a continuous process that involves every employee. By making small improvements every day, we can make real progress and deliver increasingly higher levels of customer satisfaction. Quality allows us to measure and compare our performance against the "best in class". It sets the standards for our support services and enables us to focus training and development on the most important areas.'

Rationalizing the approach to quality

The company identified that self-assessment would be critical to the success of its quality programmes:

- Self-assessment should involve every employee and help to organize and structure day-to-day work.
- It should make employees aware of the importance of improving performance against personal targets, as well as company goals.

Malcolm Baldrige criteria

The Malcolm Baldrige National Quality Award, introduced in the United States in 1987, provides an excellent basis for self-audit and review. It highlights areas for priority attention and provides internal and external benchmarking. The original aims of the Award programme were to promote:

- Awareness of quality as an increasingly important element in competitiveness
- Understanding of the requirements for quality excellence
- Sharing of information on successful quality strategies and the benefits to be derived from their implementation

The Award criteria are built upon seven core values and concepts:

Leadership
Information analysis
Strategic planning
Human resource development and management
Process management
Customer focus and satisfaction
Business results

The company first adopted the Malcolm Baldrige criteria as the basis for their self-assessment programme in 1992. The executive management team, led by the managing director, assumed overall responsibility for managing the programme and introduced a 6-monthly review process. As shown below, the score has improved steadily year on year.

Assessment date	Points
January 1992	200
July 1992	250
July 1993	287
July 1994	327
July 1995	369
July 1996	519

The review meeting uses the results of the self-assessment process to identify areas for improvement and establishes employee teams to implement improvement actions as part of a continuous improvement process. Improvement projects to date have included resolving supply issues, improving customer interfaces and the format of invoices.

Leadership from the top

To ensure that the self-assessment programme was perceived as strategically important, the company felt that it was important to manage the programme at board level. As well as the executive team which carries out the six-monthly review, they also established a Quality Council, which is chaired by the managing director and consists of the executive directors, to provide overall leadership and sponsorship of quality within the company. An essential part of the leadership task is to set the company mission and values and to communicate it throughout the organization so that everyone is aware of their role and responsibilities.

Delivering the mission requires a commitment to total customer satisfaction and to the pursuit of excellence. Leadership is therefore based on participation and open communication, together with recognition, reward and respect for the individual. Success is founded on the clarity of the mission and the pride it creates in personal responsibility and ownership.

The company's customer philosophy is based upon this mission and vision, so they ensure that all employees understand their role in helping to deliver that mission. They have also defined a set of key values which guide employees' actions and relationships both internally and externally:

The customer comes first   Total commitment to quality
Respect for the individual   Empowerment and responsibility
Open and honest communication   Team work makes a winning team
Recognition and reward for individual merit

Together, these values help to build a team of people committed to delivering the highest standards of customer satisfaction.

Involving all employees

Those key values apply from day one and, as soon as people join the company, they are encouraged to contribute to the quality process – one half of the induction programme is devoted to quality-related issues. When the company introduced self-assessment, they held a two-day awareness programme for all employees and published documentation explaining the benefits and operation of the programme.

They raise and maintain the visibility of the programme through continuous internal communications. As well as brochures and employee guides to explain the programme, they produced:

- Posters
- Items for noticeboards
- Suggestion pads

- Other eyecatching material to draw attention to quality throughout the company.

They also operate suggestion and recognition schemes to encourage active participation. All employees are invited to nominate and manage improvement projects – many of them cross-functional. The company provides full training and empowerment and operates a programme of recognition and reward. Through the suggestion scheme they encourage people to promote ideas that support key business objectives and award both monthly and annual prizes for the most innovative suggestions.

Employee feedback

As part of the policy of open communication, the company actively encourages feedback throughout the company:

- They conduct employee attitude surveys and develop appropriate improvement plans to act upon the recommendations of staff.
- They also conduct monthly surveys which invite 'internal customers' of a department to make comments and recommendations on the quality of service they receive.

Continuous improvement

Continuous improvement is at the heart of the company's quality programme and, to support that, they measure and analyse key processes monthly. They also aim to achieve best practice across key customer-facing activities. The company has established benchmarking relationships with a number of world-class organizations so that best practice can be shared and adapted by all.

Self-assessment based on the Malcolm Baldridge criteria reinforces the programme further. The company continually assesses its activities against this widely used model and use it as the basis for a programme of continuous business improvement.

The bottom line

In the company's experience self-assessment is good for business. Improvements in self-assessment scores are reflected in increased profit and customer-satisfaction performance. The quality initiatives and continuous improvement programmes the company has undertaken have helped them to maintain a market-leading position, and they believe self-assessment will continue to be an integral part of their business strategy.

Success factors in self-assessment

- Utilize proven approach such as Malcolm Baldridge.
- Lead the initiative from the top.
- Focus all staff through key values and mission statements.
- Involve staff through relevant suggestion and recognition schemes.
- Provide an organized structure for quality initiatives.
- Integrate self-assessment with quality and customer-satisfaction processes.
- Link self-assessment to continuous improvement programmes.
- Track self-assessment performance against profitability and customer-satisfaction levels.

IMPROVING EMPLOYEE SUGGESTION SCHEMES

The best companies find that success depends on continuous improvement. One big idea can transform a company, but the Japanese have proved time and time again that hundreds of small ideas lead to constant improvement. Employees should be encouraged to submit ideas because they could help to transform the business. Their suggestions reinforce quality programmes and help a company achieve its objectives.

Wherever employees work in an organization, they can contribute. You need simple ideas and plenty of them.

- Once you have a good idea, make sure it works.
- When employees submit their suggestions, ask them to tell you about both the problem and its solution. While it is valuable to highlight problems, you need to have a recommended solution so that you can initiate an improvement action.
- Look at every idea you receive and evaluate it.
- Seek guidance from sales, marketing and technical specialists to see how the suggestion could be used to improve products or service to customers.
- Decide how the suggestions could be put into action.

GETTING THE MEASURE OF SERVICE

Service measures help you focus on the issues that are most important to your customers and you should use those to refine your service action plans. However, it is essential that you understand what the service measures are telling you. The following are four indicators that measure service from different perspectives:

- *Customer satisfaction*. Provides a broad picture of customer satisfaction and the importance of service issues, giving a clear focus for customer service priorities.
- *Customer feedback*. Measures satisfaction at individual customer level.
- *Complaints analysis*. Provides up-to-date information on trends and current areas for concern and allows you to react immediately to problems.
- *Service performance*. Tests your ability to meet the service standards you set and emphasizes the importance of continuous improvement.

Focusing on customer priorities

Service measures can help you to establish the most important service issues and allow you to assess and monitor your customers' perceptions of your performance on key issues. The following is an extract from the results of a customer-satisfaction survey on contract distribution services. It lists the top ten concerns of customers.

Issue	*Satisfaction %*
1 Prompt delivery	61
2 Products arrive in good condition	62
3 Charges	64
4 Attitude of delivery staff	67
5 Flexibility	64
6 Response to urgent requests	60
7 Reporting delays	67
8 Accessibility of drivers en route	72
9 Appearance of vehicles	76
10 Accuracy of invoicing	58

This example gives a valuable insight into the type and quality of service customers want from the company. These are the issues that their customers feel are important and these are the areas that the company must concentrate on if it is to strengthen its position even further.

Refining your plans

These measures help to focus on the activities that will improve service performance by building on strengths and eliminating weaknesses. The information that is available can help you refocus your priorities. It is important that you do not try to take on too much and that your goals are realistic and achievable. The following are the important factors in refining your plan:

- Use the service measures to identify priorities, concentrating specifically on issues that are important to your customers.
- Set specific, achievable objectives.
- Concentrate on continuous small, manageable improvements.
- Involve staff in developing ideas and implementing solutions.

REVIEWING SERVICE DEPARTMENT PERFORMANCE

The following is an extract from an annual review of service department performance. As the example shows, a number of measures are used, including:

- Financial performance
- Customer satisfaction performance
- External feedback.

1996 has seen improvements across a wide range of service department measures:

- the department has exceeded budget
- Customer-satisfaction performance is improving with October above target
- Repeat repair performance has improved with a very strong performance over the last three months

There have also been significant quality improvements in key areas of service activity:

- Technicians' attitude and performance has shown a marked improvement
- The new technician intake is of a much higher calibre than before

- One of the service teams has won a national 'Supervisor of the Year' award for the second year running
- We have exceeded our training objectives
- The earlier quality problems have been overcome
- We have built new levels of confidence in our testing facilities
- A new technician pay scheme has been introduced which encourages and rewards quality.

Customer-satisfaction performance

We recognize that the service department still has a long way to go and that there is considerable room for improvement. The latest figures available indicate a performance of 8.0, ahead of the objective of 7.9.

Repeat repairs

Performance has improved steadily throughout the year with a twelve-month score of 22.6, compared with the group average of 22.3. However the score for the last three months is 18.8, considerably lower than group average.

Technician quality

One of the problems facing the service department at the beginning of the year was the quality and attitude of technicians. There has been a marked improvement over the year. The poorest performers have now left and we have recruited replacements of a higher calibre. We have put a major emphasis on training and have exceeded our training objectives. The introduction of a new pay scheme has made an important contribution to the improvement. Basic salary has been increased and other elements of the scheme are related to quality and customer-satisfaction performance. One of the encouraging results of the new scheme is that technicians are taking more time to concentrate on quality. Under the old scheme, technicians tended to complete jobs as quickly as possible to earn a productivity-related bonus. This improvement in performance has also enabled us to overcome the earlier quality problems and to build new levels of confidence in our testing facilities.

Continuous improvement

The service department supervisor has won the national 'Supervisor of the Year' award for the second year running and this success reflects the excellent overall performance of the service department team throughout the year. Although we have exceeded targets in all key areas, we are looking at ways to improve our performance even further, and we are implementing a programme of continuous improvement in all service activities.

COMPETENCE SELF-ASSESSMENT

1 Describe how self-assessment could benefit your organization.
2 List the areas where self-assessment could be used.
3 Prepare a presentation outlining a programme of self-assessment.
4 Describe your organization's key values.
5 How would you obtain employee feedback on quality initiatives?
6 Prepare a programme for encouraging employee suggestions.
7 How does your organization measure the quality of customer service?
8 What are your customers' main service concerns?
9 Prepare a presentation reviewing your department's service performance.
10 Describe a programme of continuous improvement that would benefit your organization.

11 Distribution and delivery

Distributors, agents, local branches and retail outlets play a vital role in the process of getting products and services from a manufacturer or service supplier to the final customer.

- Local outlets can provide a cost-effective supplement to the supplier's direct salesforce.
- Local outlets understand their local market and can identify changing requirements quickly.
- They are aware of local competitors and can take individual actions to deal with competitive threats.
- They can respond quickly and effectively to change in the local marketplace or to specific customer requirements.

SUCCESS FACTORS IN LOCAL MARKETING

It is possible to identify a set of success factors which can be used to evaluate the potential of distribution outlets and to measure their performance. The following are the key success factors, though they are not necessarily in order of importance:

- The distributor meets customer expectations.
- There are consistent standards throughout the network.

- Staff and management are highly motivated.
- The network is responsive and flexible.
- The distributors are financially stable.
- The network provides broad market coverage.
- The staff have the skills to provide a quality service.
- The distributors are well managed.

Meeting customer expectations

By continually measuring customer-satisfaction performance, a supplier can determine whether the branch is offering the right level of service and meeting customer's changing expectations. These customer expectations may vary at national and local level, so it is important to decide which has priority.

Motivated team

Motivation is an important feature of small businesses such as dealerships or retail outlets, but that motivation must be channelled to meet the supplier's key business objectives. Distributors may be highly motivated, but if they believe the rewards are greater from other suppliers, they may not be fully committed to one particular product range. Motivation must be developed throughout the local team, because high levels of customer satisfaction depend on a quality service from every member of a team.

Responsive

The local network must be able to respond quickly to changes in business conditions. This is not simply a question of attitude, local outlets must be continuously assessing the changing needs of their customers and suppliers must be aware of both local and national changes so that they can make appropriate changes in pricing, product range, delivery and standards. Flexibility depends on good information flow between suppliers and local outlets and a rapid decision-making process which will enable both parties to respond rapidly to threats and opportunities.

Financially stable

A local outlet that is financially stable is able to provide a guaranteed long-term service to the supplier's local customers. It also has the resources to invest in business development to meet changing customer requirements for increasing standards of customer service. The supplier contributes to this by operating effective pricing and discount policies to enable the distributor to earn a reasonable margin, and by providing marketing and business support to improve turnover and profit and run an efficient business.

Broad market coverage

The local network must enable the supplier to reach his or her whole customer base cost-effectively. It must provide the right geographical coverage and also local customers with the product knowledge and quality of service they expect from the supplier. Marketing policies and participation agreements must be acceptable to the local outlet so that they are willing to implement the whole programme and enable the supplier to cover the entire market.

Skilled staff

Quality service depends on quality staff and this is a key factor in determining the success of a local network. Skilled staff can handle customer enquiries efficiently by demonstrating the right level of product knowledge. Good customer-handling skills and understanding of customer care contribute to high levels of customer satisfaction and the skills to carry out efficient service delivery across the after-sales cycle.

Well managed

Good skills don't just apply to the staff who deliver the service, effective management can ensure that the right resources are committed to the supplier's products and that the local outlet invests in an infrastructure which provides the highest quality of service to the customer and continues to deliver an efficient profitable service.

Consistent standards

A support programme succeeds when it enables the local network to deliver consistent standards of customer service at each outlet. This does not mean delivering the same standard service because the requirements of each market may vary, but delivering the key elements that affect customer satisfaction and loyalty.

A WINNING FORMULA FOR THE AFTER-MARKET

To sell a product range into the after-market, you have to convince distributors that it will be good for their business. An effective after-market product range helps distributors win business, cut their stockholding costs, increase margins and improve customer service. There are ten key factors that distinguish a good after-market range:

Flexibility
Low order quantities on any product
Wide range of pack sizes and bulk quantities

Convenience
Single source for oils, fluids and workshop consumables
Easier ordering and administration
Fewer invoices
Stock reduction
Simple range with broad coverage
All products barcoded for easier stock control
Regular deliveries
Quality
Conformance to a recognized standard such as ISO 9002 for quality customers can rely on
Branding
Distinctive quality packaging communicating a powerful brand image
Value
Premium-quality products at competitive prices
Attractive discounts linked to purchase levels
Market potential
Trade, retail and industrial sales opportunities
Support
Attractive point of sale and promotional material
Technical advice
Comprehensive product information
Service
Dedicated salesforce
Commitment
An established, growing product range
The backing of a major organization

COMPETING THROUGH MULTIPLE SERVICE LEVELS

After-sales service can be an important differentiator but when your competitors offer the same type of service, how can you distinguish yourself? Multiple service levels are the next logical step, as the parcels distribution business demonstrates.

If you order goods by mail order these days, you will probably be offered a choice of delivery options:

- Standard (which could be three or four days or longer)
- 48-hour
- Next day
- Next morning
- Same day within a guaranteed time frame.

As competition increases, the delivery times come tumbling down, but is that necessarily what the customer needs, or is it even a practical proposition? Commentators point out that guaranteed next-day delivery is fine, provided there is someone there to receive the goods. While that may not cause problems for deliveries to business premises, increasing sales to home offices or small offices can cause problems. What happens if there is no-one to collect the goods and the driver needs a signature? Does the driver try again next day, and keep on trying until delivery is successful? Does someone at the office call the customer to arrange an alternative delivery date? Either of these can be expensive options, pushing up the cost of delivery and lowering profitability.

More important, the impact of next-day delivery is lost on the customer. Increasingly, companies are offering their customers flexible delivery options and using communications to ensure that distribution is handled efficiently and profitably.

Rapid delivery is vital if the products are time-critical. Replacement parts, for example, must be delivered in the shortest possible time if a piece of equipment has broken down. Next day, or sooner, would seem to be the logical service level. But a growing number of companies are encouraging their customers to hold small stocks of replacement parts distributed through normal scheduled deliveries. The supplier helps the customer plan the required stock level and the customer pays a standard delivery charge with no premium for rush service.

When next-day or same-day delivery is essential or desirable, companies vary in the way they charge their customers. In the competitive stationery and office supplies market, many companies offer next-day delivery as standard with no premium charge for the service. They see it as a way of differentiating their service. Others offer their customers a choice of timed options, but make different charges according to the level of service provided.

Offering a superior level of service can be an important differentiator, but it is essential to ensure that the service can be maintained. Communications can help to ensure the viability and visibility. For example, many companies phone customers in advance to keep them up to date with the progress of time-critical deliveries and to ensure that the delivery will be received. This adds another level of customer service and can also help the company to deliver a more effective service by ensuring that wasted journeys are minimized.

Improving service through delivery options
Identify the delivery service required
Offer customers delivery options
Use communications to ensure that delivery levels can be maintained

MEASURING DELIVERY PERFORMANCE

Delivery performance can be a crucial factor in building overall customer satisfaction, but how many organizations see delivery as an area for customer service attention? The following is a list of customer service standards for delivery set by a leading UK manufacturer.

Ordering

■ We will answer your calls promptly.
■ When you place your order, we will agree a delivery date with you and give you an order reference number.

After ordering

■ If we are unable to meet a particular timing request, we will inform you the working day before delivery.
■ We can provide you with estimated times of arrival (ETA) from 3.30 pm on the working day before delivery.
■ Where we have given you an ETA, we will inform you of any subsequent delays immediately.
■ If you have any queries or complaints about delivery, we will respond within two working days.

Delivery

■ We will deliver to the specified location on the agreed date within the specified operating hours.
■ Any change to the agreed delivery date, due to exceptional circumstances, will be carried out in consultation with you.
■ If we need to deliver less than the agreed quantity for operational reasons, we will consult you before making any cut to an individual delivery of 10% or more.
■ We will observe any pre-agreed delivery instructions.
■ All delivery paperwork will be clear and accurate.

These delivery standards help to deliver drivers, distribution managers, administrative staff and customers on areas that are often overlooked in customer service programmes. If your company operates its own distribution fleet, assess your operations to see whether they could meet these standards. If you use contract distribution services, ask your contractor for a copy of their standards to see whether they measure up.

DON'T BLAME THE SERVICE ENGINEER

'I don't believe it. They've given me the wrong part. Those people in the warehouse, they do this every time.'

Does this sound like a familiar problem? The service engineer arrives on-site within a guaranteed call-out time and promptly leaves, unable to carry out the repair. The result – an angry customer and a frustrated service engineer who portrays his organization as inefficient and incompetent. Hardly the recipe for effective customer service, but the situation can be avoided.

Right first time

Here are some tips for ensuring that the service company gets it right first time.

- Whenever you receive a service call, try to assess the parts that are needed.
- If it is difficult to identify the parts, advise the customer and the engineer that a preliminary site visit will be needed to assess requirements.
- Where practical, use pre-packed 'service kits' to ensure that the right parts are dispatched in line with the engineer's request.

Back up the engineer

If the worst happens and the engineer still finds that the right parts have not been delivered, it is important to limit the damage and reassure the customer that the problem will be resolved quickly and efficiently.

- Provide a dedicated hotline to enable the service engineer to reorder the right parts on emergency delivery.
- Contact the customer and the engineer to advise delivery time and arrange an appointment for the engineer to call.
- Call the customer after the return visit to check that they are completely satisfied with the repair.
- Log any parts problems, monitor performance and introduce corrective actions to improve any bottlenecks or recurring problems.

Motivate support staff

Back-up like this will help to reassure both the engineer and the customer that support staff really are committed to customer satisfaction. It is vital that support staff understand that the quality of service ultimately depends on them. Staff who just pick parts from the shelf probably don't realize how important their role is.

- Tell them about the problems on the customer site.
- Develop a bonus scheme related to quality performance.
- Involve them in improvement programmes.

Build team spirit

The quote at the beginning of this section illustrates the reaction that can take place when a service engineer feels let down by colleagues. This frustration can come across to the customer and that does little to build confidence in the supplier. The engineer probably spends more time in direct contact with the customer than staff who specialize in 'managing' customer relations.

THE DIRECT ROUTE

Increasingly, companies in sectors such as financial services and computers are adopting a 'direct' approach and selling directly to customers rather than through retailers or distributors.

First Direct

When First Direct introduced round-the-clock telephone banking it was a breakthrough in customer service. Customers enjoy a personal service whenever they choose to do business and they can carry out transactions without visiting a branch. First Direct utilized the power of database information and communications to improve personal service beyond what was available from the rest of the high street banking system. As well as improving customer service, they were also opening profitable new marketing channels.

Technology had been used to automate many traditional banking processes and the result had been a reduction in personal contact and a loss of identity. Automatic tellers, direct debits and other forms of automation meant that customers no longer needed to visit their branch. Although that might have increased efficiency and allowed the banks to improve their productivity and reduce costs, it meant that they had lost contact with their customers.

There is a parallel in the insurance business where companies had traditionally maintained a field force of collectors and agents calling on households. Direct debits and other forms of automated payment enabled the insurance company to reduce their overheads but lose vital contact. First Direct's use of technology was innovative in the finance sector. Banks and building societies had invested heavily in information technology (IT) as a means of improving productivity. At one level, IT was seen as a way of freeing staff to deal with customers; there was a clear distinction between front- and back-office duties and IT was seen as a way of dealing with the back-office issues.

This enabled banks and building societies to open up the traditional counter area to give staff and customers the chance to meet in a more personal environment. Cash dispensers and other automated processes helped customers deal with routine transactions and freed the counter staff to concentrate on customer queries, loans and other services. This trend is in line with the long-term business strategy of offering customers a wider portfolio of financial services, including insurance, mortgages, investment advice, stocks and shares, and financial advice with the aim of building customers for life.

By providing customers with cash dispensers, increased levels of direct debiting and other facilities for automated transactions, customers had less reason for visiting a branch, and contact was reduced rather than increased. Many customers felt that they were simply account numbers and that personal service was a thing of the past. First Direct focused clearly on what it saw were the customers' real needs – a personal service at a convenient time for the customer, with a high degree of flexibility. The concept was simple – 24-hour banking by telephone. A customer rings up at any time and is able to carry out a wide range of transactions over the telephone. Far from being an impersonal telephone service, the First Direct contact was perceived as a friendly and personal service where the customer was treated as an individual, rather than a number.

Role of the database

The key to effective 'direct' sales activities is the database. At minimum it should contain the following information:

- Name
- Address
- Account number
- Purchase history
- Preferences/special requirements
- Products and services bought
- Frequency of purchase
- Contact history.

Once the database is established it can be used for the following activities:

- Identifying likely purchasing patterns
- Analysing customer information as a means of cross-selling other products and services
- Assessing the effectiveness of marketing programmes

The database enables the telephone staff to handle incoming callers efficiently and identify opportunities for marketing other services. For example, the database can identify prospects for services such as life assurance, services or loans. When a customer calls, the screen prompts the operator to mention any relevant products. The customer's response is logged and the system then prompts follow-up action such as mailing further information or offering a quotation. This process can then be tracked until the prospect buys the product.

Applying the direct approach

The 'direct' approach is now being found in a number of other markets and it can be used to meet different scenarios where:

- Customers carry out specific transactions which do not depend on specialist skills.
- Computers provide all the customer information necessary to carry out transactions. Customer details are held on personal computer and can be accessed by any member of the telephone team.
- The customer sees convenience as an important aspect of the service and this convenience is not available through other forms of service delivery. In this case, customers would have to visit a branch, they may not have time or the location could be difficult.
- The service can be positioned as prompt, flexible and personal and can be tailored to the needs of individual customers.
- Quality of personal service is seen as more important than location.
- People and resources can be concentrated in specific areas, rather than scattered around a branch network.
- The service does not have to be located in a particular area and it does not have to be situated near the mechanism for delivering the service; for example, telephone banking does not require a high street location.
- The service can be branded although it has no physical existence for the customer. This runs contrary to the traditional feeling of the banks that oak panel and marble were essential to the image of stability they wished to convey.

In setting up a service like this, there are a number of important considerations:

- Deliver a quality service to the customer.
- Offer the customer maximum convenience.
- Provide customers with a prompt, flexible service.
- Utilize the power and flexibility of the database and the telephone to deliver a personal service.
- Compete effectively with traditional methods of service delivery.

Direct Line Insurance

Direct Line Insurance carved out a profitable niche in the car insurance market by offering customers a highly efficient telesales and claims-handling operation. Rather than contact a broker or a traditional insurance company direct the customer was able to benefit from a professional, no-frills operation. By reducing its overheads and not having to support a salesforce or a branch network, the company was able to offer an extremely competitive service. When prospects called, their enquiry was handled by trained sales staff who worked through a planned sequence of questions to ensure the customer received an accurate quote. The quote was handled on computer and was immediate. If the customer accepted the quote, the policy was immediately put into effect and no further action was needed.

Claims were handled in the same straightforward way. The customer phoned in, described the incident and the claim would be dealt with rapidly. This standard of service enabled Direct Line to post good profits and set a standard that other insurance companies tried to follow. The Direct Line database enabled telesales staff to streamline the process of handling enquiries by providing prompts for information. The company is now using its customer database to market a range of related financial services products, using the same customer proposition of speedy customer service.

Benefits of the direct approach

Putting the programme into operation provided important benefits for both client and service provider. Customers had a service that was focused on their needs:

- The service provided the highest levels of convenience and flexibility.
- Customers could deal with their financial affairs in the most convenient way.
- They were able to have access to a personal adviser who could deal with any aspect of their financial affairs.
- Financial affairs could be handled at times that were convenient to the customer.

■ Customers could make transactions and get an immediate picture of their situation.

The benefits to the provider were equally important:

■ They were able to reach a new market who were looking for a specific type of service.
■ They could take advantage of technology to deliver a highly efficient service.
■ They could concentrate their resources by utilizing technology to deliver a consistent nationwide service to every customer.
■ The investment in technology and communications set up strong entry barriers that deterred competition.

ADVANCED COMMUNICATIONS KEEP THE CUSTOMER INFORMED

Increasingly, companies are finding that efficient distribution is an important factor in building and maintaining customer satisfaction. Effective communications using mobile data, voice communications and vehicle tracking enables distribution managers to monitor their distribution operations and keep customers fully informed on the status of deliveries. This allows the customer to operate a more flexible stockholding operation and plan manufacturing operations more accurately.

Computer-aided dispatching, available from mobile communications specialists, increases productivity, reduces costs and improves customer service even further. Automating job allocation and dispatch frees staff, reduces paperwork and improves the quality of management information. The dispatching systems use short data messages to exchange information on the status of deliveries between an office and a vehicle. Drivers can use pre-programmed messages to report:

■ When they are approaching customers' premises
■ When deliveries have been completed
■ If any delays are likely.

Distribution controllers can keep customers fully informed and can also easily rearrange deliveries to meet changing circumstances. Vehicle tracking, using satellite geographical positioning systems, extends control even further and can be integrated with 'traffic' systems to anticipate delays and alert drivers to potential problems.

Research by psychologists into customer care found that customers do not worry unduly about delays provided they are kept informed. The information available from communications systems like this can be used to enhance the working relationship.

A component distributor supplying a large accident repair centre developed a proactive form of delivery reporting to help the repair centre enhance its own working methods. Twice a day the repair centre team met to plan the work in hand for the next shift. The supplier sent an update on all deliveries by electronic mail in time for the meeting so that the teams could identify any jobs that might be affected by late delivery of components. Communications are being used to strengthen a partnership between supplier and customer.

COMPETENCE SELF-ASSESSMENT

1 How important are local outlets to your business?
2 What are the success factors in your local outlets?
3 How can you improve those success factors?
4 Describe how your organization's product range meets your distributors' requirements.
5 Prepare a plan for applying service levels to your key after-sales services.
6 Describe the customer service standards that should be applied to your delivery operations.
7 Prepare a plan for ensuring effective parts support for service engineers.
8 How could the 'direct approach' be applied to your business?
9 Describe the key success factors in your 'direct approach'.
10 How would a direct approach work alongside traditional distribution channels?

12 Customer communications

Dialogue enables us to communicate information to our customers and get feedback from them so that we can help them make informed purchasing decisions in our favour. This chapter explains different types of internal and external communications methods and describes how to use appropriate techniques. It will help make your communications more effective by showing you how to develop an understanding of what your audience needs to know to make a purchasing decision. This chapter also explains the importance of regular communications with your customers. It stresses the importance of carrying out regular communications audits to see how well key decision makers understand you and describes a number of techniques for maintaining contact, including:

- Direct marketing
- Product updates
- Technical/research updates
- Customer team briefings on corporate progress
- Corporate/financial information
- Company direction
- Customer-satisfaction surveys
- Customer-performance review meetings
- Customer account team manuals

CARRYING OUT A COMMUNICATIONS AUDIT

The following is an audit of the planned and current communications between an information systems company and its largest client. It is concerned with the relationship and image of the supplier from the customer's point of view. It compares the customer's views with those of the supplier and incorporates the customer's views of competitors. The audit compares the actual perceptions against current communications activities and highlights key communications actions needed to achieve the target perception.

Summary of audit

The following is the management summary of the findings of the audit. The company is setting out to improve the value, market share and quality of its business with this key account, increasing market share from 19% to 25%. To achieve this, the company must secure strategic supplier status and enter a significant collaboration agreement with the customer.

Over the last year the company has improved its image within the key account, but competitors have made further gains. In certain areas the company is highly regarded, but research shows that the customer's senior managers are not aware of the company's current improvement programme. At worst, this means that the company may not be considered for certain major projects and, at best, the company may start at a disadvantage compared with its competitors. The company needs to develop a preference for its products and services, especially in the key areas identified for future business. A strong image development programme will be required to change the attitudes of the customer's senior management team.

The following is a summary of the company's current image position:

- The company is almost as 'visible' as its competitors, but is rated only third in all issues associated with image.
- Contact with the customer at all levels is less than professional. According to the customer, the company does not understand its business and its products, and does not communicate its future strategies.
- There is a legacy of poor reputation which has largely been overcome by increased product reliability, but the image persists in the minds of the customer's senior management team.
- The company is perceived as offering lower quality and lower performance than competitors, and users are less satisfied than competitive users.
- The company is seen as losing ground with important decision makers.

- The company is identified more clearly than competitors with specific product lines, but is not rated most highly as the potential supplier of those products.
- The company's major weakness is perceived as its narrow product line and lack of expertise in certain areas.

From an image development point of view, there are three major actions needed to ensure future success:

- The reality of improved performance, reliability and value for money must be sustained and improved.
- The professionalism of the company's staff, their knowledge of their products and understanding of the customer's needs must be improved. The quality and effectiveness of all contacts with the customer must be improved dramatically.
- A positive, well-managed and consistent image-development programme must be put in place to publicize the company's progress to close the gap between perception and reality and to create a preference for the company by presenting the right messages to the right members of the management team.

Changing perceptions

The major perceptions which must be created to achieve the business goals are:

- The company is a professional organization which understands the customer's business needs and can meet them with a wide range of high-quality products and services.
- The company is technically successful in major projects, developing total solutions and delivering value for money, on time, every time.
- The company is winning share from its competitors.
- The company is an approved and respected strategic supplier with whom it is safe to place business.
- The company is successful and financially stable with a sound management team – a good prospective supplier and business partner.

Communicating professionalism

'The company is a professional organization which understands the customer's business needs and can meet them with a wide range of high-quality products and services.' The messages to support this perception include:

- The company is investing £x in training over the next year.
- The company is organized into market-focused groups to offer the highest standards of service.
- x staff are dedicated to the customer's business.
- The company is committed to total quality.
- The company has developed a broad product range and a full range of support services.
- The company's products meet international standards.
- The new product development programme is providing innovative new products.

Communicating technical success

'The company is technically successful in major projects, developing total solutions and delivering value for money, on time, every time.' The important messages to support this perception include:

- The company has an established reputation for innovation.
- The company's products have been selected for the following demanding applications . . .
- Customers are saving money by using the company's products.
- The company's products conform to international standards.
- The company has a research and development budget in excess of £x and has a team of y highly skilled people dedicated to technical support.

Communicating market success

'The company is winning share from its competitors.' The important messages to support this perception include:

- The company has been selected to provide products and services to the following customers . . .
- The company has recently won a major order worth £x.
- The company has been selected as a strategic supplier to the following customers . . .
- The company has gained x% market share in the last year, while competitors have lost y% share in the last year.

Communicating strategic supplier status

'The company is an approved and respected strategic supplier with whom it is safe to place business.' The important messages to support this perception include:

- The company has been selected as a strategic supplier to the following market-leading customers . . .
- The company is collaborating with a major international organization.
- 'The company meets the following international product and quality standards . . .

Communicating corporate stability

'The company is successful and financially stable with a sound management team – a good prospective supplier and business partner.' The important messages to support this perception include:

- The company's annual results show x% growth in orders, revenue and profits.
- The company is expanding.
- The company is a member of the Y international group.
- The company is the leading European supplier.

The audit has identified the key areas for improving communications performance and it is essential that these messages should be communicated consistently in every form of contact with the customer.

COMMUNICATIONS STRATEGY

Direct marketing

Direct marketing is used to send targeted communications to named individuals. On a key account, these might be important members of the decision-making team who cannot be contacted directly or who require specific information. Direct marketing can take the form of direct mail letters, brochures, management guides or other publications that meet the reader's main concerns. Direct marketing can also be used to make special promotional offers to named individuals – invitations to seminars, offers of reprints of technical articles, free copies of business briefing guides and other items that enhance your credibility as a supplier. A direct marketing programme is based on planned, regular communications to ensure that each decision maker holds a favourable perception of your company. A programme targeting the technical director aims to position the company as an innovative, technically advanced supplier. The programme might include:

- Reprints of published articles by technical specialists on your staff
- A briefing and update on your latest research programme
- An independent review of your product performance
- Invitations to a seminar sponsored by your company on industry developments

By looking at the information requirements of the key decision makers, you can develop a comprehensive direct marketing programme.

Product updates

It is vital that your customers' technical and purchasing specialists always have the latest information on your products. This is not only sound engineering practice, it alerts them to any new developments that may help them to develop their own products. You can use a formal system of change control to ensure that each of your contacts is kept up to date.

Technical/research updates

These are similar to product updates, but they notify your customers of future developments so that they can incorporate new technology into their own forward programmes. This type of update not only enhances your technical reputation, it also helps to build closer working relationships between the technical groups. These updates can be published occasionally or at regular intervals, say quarterly or annually.

Customer team briefings on corporate progress

Significant developments such as new investment programmes, acquisitions, changes in management, expansion programmes or new product launches are of major interest to your key account customers. By bringing together the two teams, you can take the opportunity to update everyone of the progress and ensure that there are experts on hand to deal with specific issues.

Corporate/financial information

Although financial information is an integral element of the team briefing process, you can keep individual decision makers up to date by sending copies of corporate brochures, financial results and other corporate information. A regular flow of information will ensure that key influencers are aware of your financial performance and remain confident of your ability as a stable supplier.

Company direction

It is important that your key customers understand the future direction of your company – how do you see your business in the medium and long term, what new developments do you plan to introduce, and are you considering any fundamental changes to your business? Customers need to be convinced that you will remain committed to the success of their business and that they will continue to benefit from working closely with you. An understanding of your future direction helps your customers plan their own development.

Customer-satisfaction surveys

As well as keeping customers informed of developments in your company, it is also important to monitor their attitudes to your company and your performance on their account. Customer-satisfaction surveys are covered in more detail later in this book, but they should be an integral element of a two-way communications strategy.

Customer-performance review meetings

As well as measuring customer satisfaction, you should be prepared to review your performance with your key customers and discuss measures for improving performance. By taking a proactive attitude to performance measurement, you demonstrate high levels of customer care and improve relationships with team members. Review meetings can be held at a number of different levels:

- Monthly progress meetings on technical and commercial matters, involving specialist members of the team
- Quarterly review meetings on overall performance. Most of the team will participate and the meeting will be used to identify any remedial actions needed
- Annual reviews involving senior members of the team to review performance and discuss key objectives for the coming year.

Customer account team manuals

In a key account environment where a large number of people are involved, an account team manual can be extremely useful. The manual should include all the information needed to operate the account, and would be distributed to members of both teams. The contents of the manual might include:

- Introductory section on the general benefits of working together, focusing on the opportunities to improve business performance and maintain a competitive edge
- The key performance measurements used to assess progress
- The scope of the account relationship, including supply and distribution arrangements, action programmes and levels of technical and marketing cooperation
- An outline of the direction in which the account could develop, including a growth path and possible action programmes
- The quality processes and feedback mechanisms that would be used to control the programme
- The skills and resources of both companies
- The organization of the two companies, including appropriate personnel details
- The responsibilities of both parties and the reporting procedures
- Contact information explaining the communications links between the two companies and the sources of information within each
- Escalation procedures to deal with any problems on the account
- A summary of the main benefits and long-term objectives of the account relationship.

The manual is a valuable technique for building understanding and maintaining relationships between the two parties. It ensures that everyone understands their role and shows how the relationship can be utilized to provide benefits for both parties.

INCREASING CONTACT WITH PROSPECTIVE CUSTOMERS

Organizations need to ensure that they can maintain effective contact with prospects and customers. Recruiting new customers is an ongoing process and it takes time to raise the profile of an organization. Below are some ideas to help you contact prospective customers.

Make sure customers want to recommend you

Many of the best introductions come from existing customers. It is essential that customers are impressed by the quality of service they receive from all staff in the organization because this will encourage them to recommend your organization.

Impress customers with service

Research shows that a high percentage of new business comes from an existing customer base. It is essential to impress customers with service to ensure that they continue to choose you.

Make sure you have a presence at events

Many opportunities for business development come from maintaining a consistently high profile in the marketplace. By making prospects and customers aware of your interest in their business, you can help to encourage enquiries and reinforce the impact of marketing promotions.

Maintain contact with key business influencers

Accountants, solicitors and other professionals such as estate agents or surveyors can provide you with valuable contacts. Let them know about the types of customers you are targeting and ensure that they have appropriate information on your products and services.

Identify prospects through the press

The press can be a good source for identifying potential new leads. The following sections can be valuable:

- Business news
- Business advertisements
- Feature articles or advertorials contributed by local businesses

DON'T FORGET TO TELL THE WINNER

A company who managed fleet petrol costs through a company charge card operated an incentive programme for petrol retailers to sign up more card holders in their local market. Although the company dealt with major fleets at a corporate level, they were keen to build business with smaller local fleets using the retailers as a gateway.

The company magazine published a regular report on the prizes awarded to successful retailers who had signed up most new customers. Yet when the manager of one of the country's most successful retailers was approached for comments on the programme, he claimed that he was not aware his outlet had won a prize. He said that he was never told whether any of the application forms he returned had been converted to live accounts, and he found the whole scheme to be a 'nuisance'.

Clearly, this manager was not motivated to succeed, even though he was running one of the most successful outlets in the network. How much more successful would the incentive programme have been if the card operator had:

- Sent a personal letter congratulating the winners
- Issued a management report to each outlet listing the converted applications
- Issued an analysis of the business generated from each outlet's cards.

This would have ensured that the manager perceived a return for his efforts in marketing the card to potential customers – a return in both personal and business terms.

KEEPING YOUR CUSTOMERS INFORMED

How well do your regular customers know you? Do you keep them up to date with developments in your business, or do you just take it for granted that they will know all about you?

Sometimes long-term relationships can be too 'cosy' and the communications channels dry up. But what happens if competitive activity increases or the key client contact moves? It is important to treat existing clients as prospects and keep them fully informed on the service you are offering.

The official letter

You receive an official letter asking you to tender for business. It's not, as you might expect, a letter from a company that you haven't dealt with before, but one of your longest-standing customers – a company that you have dealt with successfully for over twenty years.

The tender document asks you for prices, which is okay, you think. It also asks for brief details of your company, and that's when you begin to worry. When you have worked with a company for more than twenty years, you assume they know about you.

Do your customers really know you?

When you have been working with a customer for that long, there is a risk that you take the relationship for granted.

- You don't keep customers up to date with developments in your company – it may have changed dramatically.
- You don't remind customers of the real benefits of doing business with you – there have been no complaints so you assume everything is all right.

- You may not maintain contact with some of the newer decision makers – after all you have had a good personal relationship with the same contact for many years.
- You may not be aware of competitive actions.
- You may not be aware of changes in the customer's organization – that could have implications for the business.

The risks

The arrival of this tender should alert you to a number of risks:

- Your contact may have less influence and other decision makers may not understand the full benefits of your service.
- The company may be putting an emphasis on purchasing factors that you are not aware of.
- Your competitors may be strengthening their position.
- The company may be assessing suppliers on price alone, whereas the total service you have built up offers greater value for money and may save your customers money in other areas.

Responding to the risk

You have a strong position and you must build on that, but you must also find out who is making the decision and what factors they will be assessing. You should take the following action immediately. Ask for a meeting with your main contact to find out why the tender has been sent and what are the real requirements. Try to identify all the important decision makers and ensure that you contact each of them directly or indirectly. Submit a detailed document with the tender describing the full benefits of your long-term relationship with the customer.

Maintaining the relationship

Assuming that your tender is successful, how can you ensure that you maintain a secure position with that customer? An individual customer communications plan is essential. The following are the main elements:

1 Send company information to all decision makers.
2 Send your annual report to all decision makers.
3 Arrange a regular briefing meeting (quarterly or every six months) to bring decision makers up to date with developments in your company and review any issues or problems.
4 Send information on any new developments that benefit the customer.

CAN YOU SEND ME SOME LITERATURE?

Is product literature something you just give away or could you use it to improve relations with customers? A civil servant took early retirement and decided to invest a lump-sum payment with a financial institution. He called or wrote to six institutions advertising in the personal finance section of a Sunday newspaper. The three companies that he telephoned responded in different ways:

- One asked for his address.
- One took his address and asked how much he wanted to invest.
- One asked about his plans and current situation and suggested a meeting with a consultant.

When the literature arrived, it reflected the pattern of the telephone response.

- The first 'parcel' contained every piece of literature produced by the institution.
- The second contained a selection of investment brochures aimed at the investor's own income bracket.
- The third provided an overview of the relevant options available, a reply card to request specific items of literature and a freephone number to arrange an appointment with a consultant.

The postal responses followed a similar pattern.

- The first two institutions mailed general literature 'parcels'.
- The third responded to the initial coupon by telephoning the investor and asking about his requirements before sending a tailored literature package

Mechanical process or customer relationship

When the investor had received all the literature, he was faced with a difficult choice. Should he choose the institutions which had the resources to send him a large sumptuous literature pack or should he deal with an institution that was interested in his specific needs? His preference was for the tailored approach. He wanted to deal with an institution that did not simply respond to a request for literature, but treated him as an individual from the outset.

Making the most of literature requests

How can you ensure that this approach works?

- Provide prospects with a simple response mechanism – freepost or freephone.
- With postal responses, include a coupon for capturing essential data.
- Follow up postal requests with a phone call to obtain a more detailed profile of the customer's needs.
- Only send literature that is relevant to the customer.
- Offer the customer a contact point for further advice and information.
- Try to arrange a sales appointment to move the prospect further along the decision-making process.

Copy for sample coupon

Name .... Position ....
Company .... Address ....
Telephone ....

Please send me product literature   ☐
Please telephone me to discuss my requirements   ☐
Please ask a representative to arrange a meeting   ☐

IMPROVING THE VALUE OF LITERATURE

How does literature help to generate sales and how can you improve performance? There are four steps in the process:

- Run a press advertisement including a coupon.
- Follow up the enquiry.
- Arrange a meeting.
- Make a sale.

Take a look at recent campaigns you have run:

- How many enquiries did you receive?
- How many did you follow up?
- How many meetings were arranged?
- How many sales were completed?

If you are surprised at the results, look at each of the four steps in the process again and make sure you take full advantage of your literature programme.

THREE STEPS TO SPEEDING UP INFORMATION DISTRIBUTION

Do your customers always ask for up-to-date technical or product information in a hurry? You could spend a fortune setting up distribution channels or using express post. Fax could be the answer. The following are three essential stages:

1 Design your product information to a format that can be easily faxed – single sheet, minimal illustrations, plenty of sub-headings to guide the reader, and a clear typeface that will still be legible even after faxing.
2 Use your own fax to circulate information to your customers or use a fax bureau for large-scale distribution.
3 Consider setting up a 'fax on demand' programme. Customers respond to a series of telephone messages originated from a computer and use their telephone keypad to enter codes for the appropriate literature and their own fax number. The information is sent back automatically to the caller's fax number.

COMPETENCE SELF-ASSESSMENT

1 Carry out a communications audit for your organization.
2 What does the audit tell you about customer perceptions of your organization?
3 Describe the key communications requirements for your department and your organization.
4 Which aspects of your organization's performance should be emphasized in a communications programme?
5 Prepare a communications plan for your organization.
6 Describe how you would maintain effective contact with your most important customers.
7 Describe how you would speed up information distribution.

13 Customer relationships

Keeping the customers you have is essential, because replacing them is not going to be easy. However, there are two important questions.

- Is it really sensible to keep as many customers as possible?
- Should retention activities take precedence over customer-acquisition programmes?

The answers are NO and NO. By understanding your customers' lifetime value, you can be selective about who you try to keep, as well as who you try to attract.

The bottom line
A 5% increase in customer retention could create a 125% increase in profits.
A 10% increase in retailer retention can translate to a 20% increase in sales.
Extending customer lifecycles by 3 years could treble profits per customer.

CUSTOMER LIFETIME VALUE

Customer lifetime value is exactly what it says it is – it is how much your customers are worth to you over the length of time that they are your customers. It is important to realize that worth means profitability, not spend.

For example, the bank customer who has a high monthly salary paid into his account each month, but immediately transfers spare funds into his building society account and takes out a car loan with another organization is not worth a lot to his bank.

The lifetime for customers will vary from industry to industry and from brand to brand within a single organization. You can assume that the lifetime of customers has come to an end when their contribution becomes so small as to be insignificant, unless, of course, you take steps to revitalize them.

A good customer is a long-term one who regularly buys a profitable product and who has bought recently. A new customer may be the best customer of all since their lifetime value has yet to be realized. An old customer who does not buy regularly, and has not bought recently, is probably not a customer at all. A lapsed customer who has been re-recruited often behaves like a new customer.

Lifetime ambitions – getting the most from your customers

Calculating lifetime value is just the starting point for profitable customer relationships. How can you make the make the most of lifetime customers? The core product may not be sufficient as the following example from the finance sector shows.

Lifetime potential of a financial services customer

Current account	Savings account
Personal loans	Mortgage
Life assurance	Pension
Investment advice	Taxation services

WELCOMING NEW CUSTOMERS

What happens when a customer has bought a high-value product or service? Do you follow up the sale or simply ignore the customer and rely on advertising to bring them back for the next purchase? An international telecommunications company produces a special welcome pack which thanks the customer for choosing the company and explains how the customer can get the best from the company's services. The welcome pack includes:

■   A letter from the customer service representative
■   A guide to contacting the company with queries
■   Information on the company and its services
■   A guide to using the services

Welcoming letter

This letter thanks the customer for choosing the company and gives the customer a point of contact for any queries. It also explains that the representative will be in touch with you regularly to ensure that the customer is satisfied with the service and to keep the customer up to date with developments.

Personalized calling card

The customer is issued with a calling card which can be used to contact the company with any queries or service requests. It includes a special freephone number and customer-identification number. The freephone number puts the customer straight through to a member of the Customer Service team.

The customer is asked to quote the unique identification number whenever they contact the company with any queries or service requests. The customer number helps staff to have account information and service records to hand so that they can deal with the call promptly.

Single point of contact

The freephone number provides a convenient, single point of contact for all services. A member of the Customer Service team will take the call and establish the customer's exact requirements. If the Customer Service representative cannot deal with the enquiry, the customer is transferred to an appropriate specialist. The welcome pack advises the customer of the services that are available, including:

■   Technical queries
■   Service requests
■   Customer service
■   Order processing
■   Invoice queries
■   Helpline general queries
■   Product information

Company information

The welcome pack includes a brief profile of the company to reassure the customer that they have chosen a reliable supplier. If the customer wants more information, they are asked to contact the Customer Service representative or ask for a copy of the company's corporate brochure. The following example is typical of the information that could be included.

The company at a glance

- Part of one of the world's leading telecommunications companies with more than x employees
- One of the leading communications providers in North America
- Carrying over 4 million hours of traffic per week across more than 1 million lines
- More than 1 million customers
- Sophisticated digital network incorporating satellite and fibre optics
- Support and service around the clock
- Innovative product range
- Committed to the highest standards of customer satisfaction

Customer commitment

The company outlines its commitment to the customer and explains the standards of service the customer can expect.

We will provide you with telecommunications solutions that take your business forward.
We aim to achieve the highest levels of customer satisfaction.
We will deliver a personal service through a dedicated customer service team/representative.
We will continue to develop innovative, practical solutions that reflect your real business needs.
We will provide you with advice and guidance to help you take full advantage of access to our global digital network.
We will provide you with convenient, timely billing systems that keep you in control of your telecommunications costs.
We will offer you sophisticated call information to help you plan and control your business more effectively.
We will offer you the benefits of our accumulated experience with millions of satisfied customers worldwide.
We will manage our business efficiently and responsibly so that we continue to provide you with a viable, profitable long-term partnership.

Reinforcing the benefits of the service

The welcome pack provides an opportunity to reinforce the benefits of the service and encourages the customer to make full use of those services. The customer can:

- Make calls anywhere in the world, any time, quickly and easily
- Enjoy clear call quality and rapid connections
- Improve the standards of service to your customers and your staff
- Enjoy the highest levels of reliability
- Take advantage of the latest developments in telecommunications and emerging technologies

Introduce other services

The welcome pack also provides an opportunity to cross-sell other products and services. In the example below, the product benefits are presented in relation to the customer's business.

Increase your responsiveness with more lines

Suppose you find you need more lines to handle increasing traffic. Just contact us and, within hours, we can provide you with the extra lines. You can maintain and enhance the level of service to your customers with ease.

Enhance security and service with Call Line Identification

You can also take advantage of Call Line Identification (CLI). CLI is a service that enables your staff to identify the caller before answering the call. It improves customer service, security and can also be used to improve call handling. CLI ensures that calls are routed to the most appropriate staff and can be used in conjunction with Computer Telephony Interface (CTI) to provide individual customer information on a personal computer screen. This improves the efficiency of telephone order processing or the handling of enquiries and allows staff to deliver a more personal service.

Helping the customer evaluate products and services

To help the customer identify areas of the business where the company's products and services could help them improve business, the welcome pack includes a self-assessment questionnaire. If the customer wishes to review any of the issues in more detail, they are invited to contact the Customer Service representative to arrange a meeting.

Improving customer service

Question   *Possible solution*

Do you want to make it easier for
customers to dial direct to specific
members of staff?
Do you want to encourage
customers to make greater use of
your support services?
Do you want to extend your
'opening hours' without increasing
staffing levels?
Do you want to make it easier for
customers to reach sales staff on
the move?
Do you want to simplify literature
requests?

Keeping in contact with the customer

The company promises to maintain regular contact to ensure that the service
continues to meets the customer's requirements. The Account Manager arranges
to meet the customer once a quarter to review the account and the company also
agrees to keep the customer informed of any technical or product updates or of
any significant changes in the business.

The welcome pack lays a good foundation for future relationships with
the customer and helps to build customer satisfaction from the outset.

FOLLOW UP THAT SALE

When a customer leaves the showroom, how quickly does the impact of the new
product wear off? What happens if the customer discovers a problem? How can
you reinforce the customer's loyalty from day one?

Make a courtesy call

A few days after customers have taken delivery of the product, call up to ask
them how they found the product. Are they still pleased with their choice? Does
it do what they expect? Do they need any help in using the product? Are there
any unexpected problems? The same approach can be used after a service or
repair. Is the fault cured or the product performing better? Was the customer
completely satisfied with the way the service was carried out?

Send a letter

Sometimes a letter may have more impact than a phone call, particularly if it is a personal letter from someone senior in the company. The letter would cover the same points as the phone call and would invite the customer to call the senior manager personally if there were any concerns. Although this approach is less personal than a phone call, customers may feel it is less obtrusive. A letter also gives the customer time to think about a reply and this may be more acceptable.

Send a questionnaire

You can ask the customer even more about the purchase and the product by sending a questionnaire. How do they find the product? Were they pleased with the service they got? Do they wish to make any comments about the service? A questionnaire is the least personal of the three approaches and you may not get a very high response, but the information can be valuable in identifying possible weaknesses in the sales process. The following is an example of a questionnaire from a retail outlet to customers who have bought consumer durable products.

'Thank you for sparing a few minutes to fill in our customer service questionnaire. Your responses are of great value to us in identifying areas where we can improve our service to you. When you have completed the form please return it in the stamped addressed envelope provided.'

1   While you were in the showroom did a member of staff acknowledge you?
2   Did the sales person introduce themselves?
3   Which of the following questions did the salesperson ask?
    Style/range required
    Budget
    Accessories required
4   Did the salesperson provide any of the following?
    Brochure
    Details of the guarante
    Price
    Business card

5   How satisfied were you with the
    sales/service you received?
    Very satisfied
    Fairly satisfied
    Not satisfied
If you would like to make any further comments please
use the space below.

Send the customer details of accessories or service

It's never too soon to start selling to the new customer. The offer of accessories
that will enhance the original purchase or service to keep the product in top
condition can help to reinforce the value of the original sale. The following is an
example of a letter from a local car dealer, inviting recent car buyers to join the
Gold Club.

Welcome to the Gold Card Club

We are delighted that you have chosen to buy ... and we
hope you enjoy many years of enjoyable, trouble-free
motoring. To help you make the most of your new car, we
would like to welcome you to the Gold Card Club. When
you join, you will receive a free membership card which
entitles you to a great range of savings and benefits.

For a start, you can get 10% off all service, repair and
parts bills. When you book a scheduled service in advance,
you'll be entitled to a courtesy car. As a special introductory
bonus, we are pleased to offer you £100 worth of free
accessories. You can take advantage of this offer for up to
three months after you buy your car. Ask for our
accessories catalogue now and make your choice.

The offers don't stop there. As a privileged member,
you'll receive regular news about special membership
offers and we'll keep you up to date with developments at
our garage.

Membership is free if you have bought a new or
used car within the last four months. All you have to do is
phone ... and give us your name and date of purchase.
We'll send you your free Gold Card Club details.

PS: Don't forget to ask for an accessories catalogue and
    start choosing your £100 worth of free accessories.

Retaining customers

Activities like this are just the beginning of a programme to retain customers. Contacting the customer just after the purchase is vital, but it is equally important to maintain contact six months, a year or several years after the original purchase. Customer-retention programmes can take many different forms from simple concepts like discounts on repeat purchases, incentives for multiple purchases to more complex frequent user programmes which provide rewards for customers who continue to use a service. Customers who stay with a company can provide long-term stability. It costs less to retain existing customers than to win new ones and existing customers can be a valuable source of new business opportunities.

PERSONAL RELATIONSHIPS

Continuity of relationships can be a powerful factor in maintaining customer loyalty. Many customers express concern about the impact of personnel changes on their business relationships. They feel that continuity is important and, although you may not be able to avoid change, you can minimize risk by handling the change with professionalism and efficiency.

In any customer/supplier scenario, a change on either side can create uncertainty and a risk of trouble:

- Newcomers may not 'understand our needs'.
- The outgoing person may have built a dependent relationship which the newcomer may not be aware of.
- The customer may feel that he or she has lost a contact with a great deal of knowledge and understanding.

There are four guiding principles to help companies decide how they should handle a change in customer-facing personnel:

1   Prioritize time and effort on the basis of the customer's long-term value.
2   Be conscious of the threat of losing the customer.
3   Emphasize continuity not change in customer communications.
4   Ensure that the incoming member of the team can demonstrate an understanding of the customer's business and its needs.

A smooth handover demands a high level of cooperation between outgoing and incoming staff to ensure that the newcomer demonstrates the right level of continuity to the customer. Important actions might include:

- Training and development of product knowledge in areas that are important to the customer

- Briefing on the customer's procedures and structure
- A review of any concerns or problems expressed by the customer.

Handled properly, the introduction of a new point of contact can strengthen customer relationships.

BUILDING CUSTOMER DEPENDENCY

How can you increase your customers' dependence on you and strengthen long-term relationships? It is important to understand your customers' business goals – what is their corporate direction, how do they aim to succeed, what are their key objectives? By showing how your products or services can help them to achieve their business objectives, you demonstrate that you can make an important contribution to their business.

By putting together a dependency checklist, you can develop a plan that shows how you could strengthen relationships with your customers.

1   List the factors that are most important to your customers.
2   Describe how you could contribute to the achievement of your customer's objectives.
3   Prepare a plan for increasing your involvement with your customer.

Dependency scenarios

The following are a number of problems your customers might face. The right level of customer service and support could help them to succeed.

- Your customers want to achieve market leadership through innovation. Your technical skills and resources can help them develop the right level of innovation without investment in their own skills.
- Your customers want to become value-for-money suppliers and succeed through competitive pricing. You can help them reduce overall costs by improving design and manufacturing costs or by handling non-core activities cost effectively.
- Your customers want to increase their capacity so that they can compete effectively with larger competitors. You can supplement their resources by providing external skills and resources.
- Your customers want to develop a nationwide network of local branches. You can provide a basis for their network

through your own local resources, cutting down on their investment and giving them a rapid start.

- Your customers want to build a strong international presence. If you have an established international network, your partners can use your local knowledge and contacts to establish their international business.

- Your customers want to rationalize their operations to concentrate on their core business. They can utilize your specialist skills to supplement their resources and allow their key staff to focus on strategic business tasks.

- Your customers want to maintain their market position by strengthening their supply position. You can provide them with a quality-assured source of supply that provides them with continuity.

- Your customers want to improve the performance of their own products and services by using your design and development skills. Through partnership, they may gain privileged access to your technical skills to improve their own competitive performance.

- Your customers want to use your technical expertise to enhance the skills of their own technical staff. By working with your technical staff, they may be able to learn new skills and techniques, and broaden their own experience so that they can make a more effective contribution to their own technical operations.

- Your customers want to use your technical resources to handle product development on a sub-contract basis. This provides your partners with access to specialist resources or additional research and development capacity to improve the performance of their product-development programmes.

- Your customers want to use your technical expertise to develop new products that they could not achieve themselves. This provides them with new technology and allows them to diversify in line with your specialist skills.

- Your customers want to use your skills and experience to overcome technical problems. If they are having recurring problems with performance and reliability, your skills can help them reduce complaints and increase customer satisfaction.

- Your customers want to use your design skills to improve through-life costs. By carrying out value engineering studies on your customers' products, you may be able to reduce overall costs and improve reliability by designing components that are easier to assemble and maintain.

■ Your customers want your technical support and back-up. If they have to provide their users with a technical support service, you can supplement their resources or handle the support service on their behalf.

Assessing customer dependency

The following is a summary of the customer dependency factors. You should decide which of them are most important to your customers and assess how could you contribute to the achievement of your customer's objectives.

Achieve market leadership through innovation.
Reduce overall costs.
Increase capacity.
Develop nationwide network.
Build a strong international presence.
Concentrate on core business.
Strengthening supply position.
Improve the performance of products and services.
Enhance the skills of technical staff.
Use your technical resources.
Develop new products.
Overcome technical problems.
Improve through-life costs
Technical support and back-up.

ENSURING CUSTOMER SATISFACTION

Customer service continues long after the sale. Delivery, service, invoicing, guarantees and the response to customer complaints can all contribute to long-term customer satisfaction.

Coordination throughout the organization

When a company deals with customers through a branch network, the risk of a weak link in the chain of customer satisfaction is high. In the following example, a car hire group ran a series of regional promotions offering regular rental customers model upgrades for a limited period. Billing and customer service was handled centrally.

The offer varied by region and this proved to be a major stumbling block. Details of the model upgrades were supplied by local branches on computer, but they were not always marked as promotional offers. As a result, many customers were incorrectly billed for higher rental rates when they should have been charged at their original model rate.

Charged at the wrong rate

One large fleet customer had upgraded twelve sales representatives' cars to executive models for the promotional period. When the monthly invoice arrived it showed the executive models charged at the full rate. The customer complained to the local branch and was advised to pay the invoice at the original rate. The local branch would take care of the administration.

Demands for money owed

The next month a letter arrived from the company's accounts department pointing out that the customer owed a sum of money which was the difference between the original and promotional model figures. The customer was asked to settle the amount without delay. If there was any query, he should contact the local branch. The customer wrote to the local branch and assumed that everything was being sorted out.

The next month there was another demand for further payments at the higher rate. The customer wrote again to the local branch, including a copy of the original letter.

The end of the promotion and the relationship

Three weeks later the promotion ended and the customer returned the executive vehicles. The next day two letters arrived – one from the accounts department asking for even more money and the second offering the customer the opportunity of a longer-term upgrade for an attractive preferential rate.

The customer telephoned the local branch and politely declined the long-term offer. However, the demands at the higher rate continued to arrive until finally the customer wrote to the local showroom cancelling the entire agreement. The result – a promotional programme that had gone badly wrong and permanent damage to customer relationships.

What went wrong?

Problem	Recommendation
The branch failed to liaise effectively with accounts	Make sure that any changes in account details are notified to the accounts department correctly.
The branch failed to reply	Any customer complaint or query should be followed up immediately by telephone or letter.
The branch took no remedial action	Any query should be followed up by remedial action. The branch should have advised accounts of the customer's situation.

Failure to escalate a recurring problem

After the problem had occurred again, the branch should have replied to the customer and also asked a senior member of the company or the customer service department to contact the customer.

Lack of liaison

While a serious dispute had not been resolved, the company continued to issue promotional offers. Coordination between different branches and between head office and branches is essential.

COMPETENCE SELF-ASSESSMENT

1 Describe how you would assess the lifetime value of your customers.
2 List the full range of products and services you could sell to customers over a long-term period.
3 Prepare a plan for 'welcoming' an important new customer.
4 Prepare a statement of customer commitment for your department.
5 Assess your current methods of following up sales.
6 Prepare a questionnaire for following up sales.
7 Describe the key factors that make customers dependent on you.
8 What are the important factors in delivering customer satisfaction?
9 Prepare a checklist for evaluating customer service problems.
10 Take a list of recent customer complaints and make recommendations for improving the situation.

14 Customer service skills

We all know that dealing with people can be demanding. As you meet all types of customers, you will realize the importance of knowing a little about human behaviour. You will also realize that different situations require different responses and differing levels of skill. Educating a customer is easier than dealing with an angry customer who is dissatisfied.

It is also true to say that no two customers are alike. Customers come from different backgrounds, have different concerns, and may have different expectations. You'll need to develop both a range of communication skills and a process for successful customer service.

CARING FOR YOUR CUSTOMERS

Three basic foundation skills will enable you to succeed. They are known as *Key Principles*. They are:

1 Maintain and enhance self-esteem
2 Listen and show you understand
3 Ask for ideas and offer suggestions

Maintain and enhance self-esteem

What is self-esteem? It can be described as having a good opinion of oneself. Everyone likes to feel important and valued by others. This applies to customers and colleagues alike. Each of our customers must be made to feel that they are an important person when dealing with a representative of the company. When customers feel they are respected then they are far more willing to listen to your suggestions and the company's position.

So what does this mean in practice? It means treating customers politely, with respect and as knowledgeable people in their own right. It means not doing or saying anything to make them feel small or belittled as individuals. It means praising their suggestions and good ideas as well as showing that you and the company value them as customers.

You can do this in three ways:

- Recognize the customer's good idea or suggestion.
- When appropriate, ask the customer for ideas or suggestions.
- Focus on the problem not the individual.

One of the simplest and most effective ways of improving a person's self-esteem is by recognizing their ideas when they are useful, or actively seeking people's ideas and suggestions. Everyone likes to feel that their contributions are important. Obviously it is not possible to solve every problem straight away, but by maintaining the other person's interest, you can gain their commitment to coming up with a solution.

The key is to focus on the facts in trying to resolve the situation. When complaining about some aspect of the service, the customer may become angry, abusive, or even violent with you. In these situations, it is important to concentrate on the facts of the situation rather than the customer's personality. Getting into an argument over who is to blame will only result in more difficulties. When customers see you are concentrating on the facts their self-esteem will remain intact.

Listen and show you understand

Have you ever talked to someone you know wasn't listening? How did you feel? The chances are that if you are like most people you felt lousy. Listening is very important. When customers know that you are listening to them they are more prepared to listen to you. This will make it easier for you to get to the root of the problem and find a way to solve it.

Even if you are a good listener, you have to let people know that you've heard and understood them – what they've said and what they feel. This lets the customer know that you value them. There are several ways to show the customer that you've heard and understood. You can let them know you understand how they feel about the situation by briefly checking the details with them.

For instance, let us assume that a customer has had repeat service calls to deal with a recurring fault. You'll need to recognize that the customer will feel frustrated and annoyed. You might say something like 'I know it's annoying to have your service go down again Mr Jones. Now if you can give me some details of the problem, I will do all I can to help you.'

By calming the customer you'll find it easier to focus on the problem or concern. So, listening brings practical and personal benefits. When you listen you'll find that your customers value you more highly – that's good for your credibility and your self-esteem.

Ask for ideas or offer suggestions

When customers have problems they often have definite ideas on how to solve them. If you ask customers for their ideas you may be able to:

- Use them directly or build on them. This will enhance their self-esteem and make it easier for you to gain their cooperation.
- Explain to them why you can't use their ideas and offer your own in return. You will at least have clarified their concern.

You can also use this Key Principle by asking straightforward open questions beginning 'What, Who, Why, or When'. This will encourage the customer to identify the cause of the problem and provide you with much-needed information to solve it.

Sometimes our customers may not be able to offer ideas because they are unfamiliar with our organization or procedures, or because they do not understand their equipment. You'll need to offer some suggestions and build their self-esteem. By offering practical suggestions you and the customer can focus on solving the problem, rather than exchanging unhelpful comments.

Using this Key Principle will help you get the customer involved and working with you rather than against you. Good listening is the key to success in business and the key to successful customer service. In the absence of good listening communication often breaks down and effective, profitable business endeavours ultimately are jeopardized. What the customer is saying and what you have heard affects how the customer views your behaviour and ultimately, that of the company.

Exercises in listening

The following exercises are designed not only to help you recall the information previously studied but also provide you with a basic format to use in anticipation of a variety of situations you may encounter.

1 As a customer-facing employee, how do you effectively communicate with your customers?
2 What are the results of ineffective communication on you?
3 Name three characteristics of all telephone calls:
   a   b   c
4 List some tips which help as you listen more effectively.
5 What else, besides facts, should you listen for?
6 What is your response when a customer is unreasonably angry and uses strong language?
7 How does this affect your job performance?
8 How should you handle an unreasonable customer?
9 What information do your customers misunderstand most often?
10 What types of customers do you most often talk to?
11 Considering the variety of individuals you deal with, how would you describe the way the majority of them behave on the phone?
12 What problems do your customers call in with most often?
13 What is the disadvantage of using short cuts when handling a problem?
14 Have you encountered customers who have had the same problem over and over again? How do they feel?
15 What are the goals of each problem-solving call?
16 You have been given numerous suggestions regarding becoming a better listener. Name four or five which you consider to be the most important.

CREATING A PROFESSIONAL IMPRESSION

The price of unprofessionalism is high. Poor customer service will hit bottom-line profit in a major way. Nine out of ten people who are treated discourteously will never talk about it to the company but will instead just walk, taking their business with them. Of those people who walk, seven out of ten typically cite the way they were treated during their introduction as the main or first cause of dissatisfaction.

Research shows that when a customer has a negative experience with a company that customer will tell an average of eleven people who are not connected to the company about their experience. In turn, each of the eleven will tell five others. So now fifty-five people – all potential customers know about the negative perception. Bad news travels fast.

On the other hand, good news travels more slowly. On average satisfied customers tell only three people about their positive experiences. This means that good impressions must be more numerous than bad ones.

Top customer complaints

- Unanswered phones
- Rude service employees
- Uninformed staff
- Delayed service
- Insensitivity and apathy towards the customers' requests
- Inaccurate or unintelligible billing
- Misinformation at the point of sale

All these complaints can be avoided by acting in a professional way. Every service professional should have the skills, knowledge and a commitment to ensure that the company does not fail on these counts.

TIPS FOR TOP PROFESSIONALS

Know your industry

If you are a professional you will see it as your own responsibility to update your product knowledge on a continual basis. Moreover, you will ensure that you are aware of the latest developments in the market. You will know how your competitors are positioning themselves, what products and what prices they are offering.

Know your job

You should have a job description that outlines the key activities and performance measures in your role. Familiarize yourself with it. But remember, it is only a start point – the real job description is delivering the best quality customer service possible.

Work smarter, not harder

Professionalism means doing things the right way at the first time of asking. It means working speedily but consistently and effectively so that there is less rework. It also means doing the things that genuinely contribute to customer satisfaction and not the irrelevant peripherals.

Influence the customer

Customer service and sales representatives directly influence customers through their manner and through their ability to deliver good information which will enable the customer to make the right buying decision.

The customer buys not once but three times

The customer buys the person, then the company, and finally the product. If we cannot sell ourselves and our company then it really does not matter how good the product is.

What the customer really wants is a first-time fix

Whether the customers are buying, have a service problem or have an enquiry, they are looking for a knowledgeable response which will solve their problems. They do not want to be moved around the company in search of the right person.

EFFECTIVE CUSTOMER CONTACT

First Contact Resolution

'First Contact Resolution' means that when customers contact a company, their needs are met at the first point of contact. Further, the contact should result in the customers' feeling good about the company's ability to meet their needs.

The main customer contact points

Sales	Telemarketing
Customer service	Installation
Technical service	

Each employee in each area during each operating day contacts a significant number of customers. Each contact or transaction is the focal point for First Contact Resolution. How each contact is resolved determines what customers think about the company. A company's public image, therefore, is the result of the success or failure of every first contact experience. Customers expect reasonable access to a contact point and expect prompt resolution of their problems.

Who is responsible?

First Contact Resolution is the responsibility of everyone:

- Direct-sales representatives
- Telemarketers
- Customer service staff
- Managers.

The contact process

Now let's examine precisely what this first contact means to you as a customer contact person. It is important for you to realize, and to thoroughly understand the critical value of the initial contact. In many cases, it will be the first fifteen seconds, particularly on the phone. You have a very limited time to establish the rapport or atmosphere with the customer. There is a sequence through which all your encounters must pass. In this sequence:

- Phase one is *contact*
- Phase two is a *midterm* of varying duration
- Phase three is the ending or *goodbye*

When working with customers, it is essential that you be proficient in all three areas: knowing how to open, how to continue and how to appropriately close every customer contact situation.

The four Cs of customer contact

At the core of a good customer contact situation there are four Cs.

Confidence
Creativity
Caring
Consideration

- *Confidence* – You must convey a certain degree of self-confidence as a foundation for any successful encounter.
- *Creativity* – Being creative in making contacts means finding ways to tune into the feelings of customers.
- *Caring* – Showing the customer that you are listening and interested is the main indication that you genuinely care.
- *Consideration* – You should radiate a believable concern which makes the customer feel comfortable.

Face-to-face contact with customers

It is impossible to be in the presence of another person and not make contact. The following are a few key pointers to reinforce the weight and value of the initial contact. As human beings we are always communicating and, of the possible 100% of all communication which occurs among people, approximately 75–80% is non-verbal. Of the non-verbal communication, approximately 70–75% of that is communicated on your face. The rest is your body language.

Since you have a very short time to establish a positive rapport with a customer, you must be extremely conscious of your facial expressions because they have a tremendous impact on the customer. Do not depend only on your verbal skills or product knowledge to get you by. When in contact with a customer, remember that if you are tired, ill, crabby, angry, preoccupied, bored or whatever, it shows all over your face.

The essential customer contact skills

- *Listening* – Effective listening includes: being prepared for the conversation, learning how to resist distractions, sometimes taking notes, getting the whole picture (facts, emotions, attitudes and expectations), remaining unbiased and unemotional, and not hurrying.
- *Acknowledging* – Acknowledging includes: letting your customer know that you are listening. It is the link between listening and probing, showing empathy, illustrating that you understand them. Affirm what the customer has said in a positive manner. You use these statements to identify and acknowledge your customer's feelings. This is what encourages them to continue talking. Then, finally restate what you think is the important information stated by the customer. Be as short and concise as possible. Acknowledging, handled properly, establishes a warm, friendly, genuine tone and atmosphere. Acknowledging is good customer service.
- *Probing* – Probing ensures a productive customer contact. To do this, you need to be certain that you have all the essential information about the customers and their needs. Having listened to the customer and having acknowledged that you have heard what was said, you can now begin to probe. It is important to gather as many facts as possible and to keep control of the conversation. Probing helps you to gather information and control the conversation. In gathering information you should be able to determine the reason the customer contacted the company, identify their interests, and better understand your customer. Learning to control the conversation will be one of your most valuable skills.

Tips for effective customer contact

1 *Acknowledge the customer's presence immediately* – Whatever you are working on can wait until after the customer has been served. Do not keep them waiting. If

you are already busy with another customer, either in person or on the phone, provide some non-verbal acknowledgement that you are aware of their presence, perhaps a genuine smile or head-nod of acknowledgement.

2 *Concentrate on the customer* – When making contact with customers, look them straight In the eye and genuinely concentrate on their needs. Looking at them so directly assists you in focusing your attention. This also helps to centre your energy.

3 *Open with a friendly greeting* – Customers respond to your attitude. If you are sincere, friendly, polite, enthusiastic and use a positive tone of voice, they are more likely to respond favourably to you and to your company.

4 *Refer to customers by name* – Listen for their name. If it is not mentioned, ask for it. Then address your customer by name throughout the conversation. This technique personalizes the service and lets customers know how much your company values their business.

5 *Assure customers that you can help* – Put your customers at ease immediately by letting them know that you can help. If you assure your customers of your willingness to solve their problems or answer their questions, you will be able to proceed with the actual business of their visit more quickly.

6 *Listen to and acknowledge your customers* – Listen to determine the reason for their enquiry and to better understand the situation. By listening well, you can obtain information from your customers about their feelings and expectations. As you listen, acknowledge what your customer is saying. Acknowledging lets customers know that you hear them, that you understand how they feel and that you will take action.

7 *Ask customers questions* – In every contact, you need to be certain that you have all the required information about the customers and their situation. Asking questions will help you solve their problems, answer their questions and provide accurate information.

8 *Create realistic expectations* – Explain your services and policies in detail so your customers are comfortable with what they are buying. By creating realistic expectations, our customers will not be disappointed and will more thoroughly enjoy the service.

9 *Verify customer satisfaction* – Don't proceed without making sure that what you're doing is okay with the customer. Customers are often reluctant to speak frankly when something is wrong.

10 *Thank customers for calling* – A thank-you lets your customers know you appreciate them and their business. Also, to ensure a good long-term relationship, let your customers know you are there to help them at any time in the future.

IMPROVING THE PERFORMANCE OF CUSTOMER-FACING STAFF

Customer service staff are created, not born, although certain innate characteristics of care and empathy are important. By developing a comprehensive job specification and skills profile, you as managers can improve the performance of your customer service staff by focusing on the most important traits. The job specification should cover the following areas:

- Key responsibilities
- Contacts
- Reporting
- Measurable results
- Training requirements
- Professional and personal skills
- Experience
- Career development
- Support requirements

The following are some brief examples of customer service job specifications.

Service receptionist car dealership

- Takes telephone bookings for service and repairs
- Meets customers when they hand over their car for service/repair
- Hands back car to customer after service

Helpline operator

- Handles incoming customer queries
- Responds to straightforward queries
- Puts specialists in touch with customers for more complex queries

Account manager

- Liaises with customers
- Manages customer's business requirements within the company
- Coordinates resources used to deliver service to the customer.

Personal banker

- Liaises with customers
- Provides advice and guidance to customers
- Resolves customer queries

Distribution supervisor

- Ensures deliveries in line with customer schedules
- Coordinates distribution resources
- Deals with customers' delivery enquiries.

Personal incident manager

- Coordinates recovery services for customers whose cars have broken down
- Advises customers on personal and legal issues
- Keeps customers informed of progress on recovery.

Credit controller

- Liaises with customers over payments
- Recovers bad debts
- Advises customers on alternative methods of payment.

Service engineer

- Visits customer sites to maintain equipment
- Deals with customers' equipment queries
- Advises customers on correct equipment usage

POSITIVE TELEPHONE RESPONSE

How do your staff answer the telephone? Do they just pick up the phone and answer routinely, or do they see every phone call as an opportunity to create the right impression and improve customer service? Try our telephone self-assessment on your staff . . . you might be surprised at the results. Better still, try calling your own office without identifying yourself, and see how your staff rate against the assessment.

1 How quickly do you answer your phone?
2 How do you identify yourself? Department? Company?
3 Is your acknowledgement of the customer's opening statement appropriate?
4 Do you interrupt customers or fail to give way when they try to interrupt?
5 If the call is suspended, do you leave the line and return to the line in a polite manner?
6 Are you attentive to the customer's statements or do you ask questions which indicate you were not listening?
7 Do you express concern or regret where appropriate? Do you apologize, if necessary?
8 Do you express in words or indicate by your manner and tone of voice a willingness to be of help?
9 Is your attitude friendly, helpful and interested, or does the caller receive routine treatment instead of individual consideration?
10 When the caller requires information or an explanation, is it given completely and concisely?
11 Do you use technical terms, jargon or arbitrary phrases?
12 Do you handle calls in a manner that would convey confidence in the way your company is managed? Will the caller want to remain a customer?
13 Are the final arrangements clear?
14 Do you respond appropriately to customer's 'Thank you' or other closing remarks?
15 Do you transfer calls thoughtfully?
16 Do you plan your calls ahead?
17 Do you keep paper and pencil handy?
18 Do you wait for the other party to hang up first?
19 Do you hang up your phone securely?
20 Do you dread the next call?

WORKING WITH DIFFICULT CUSTOMERS

To satisfy a customer you need to do whatever it takes. So employees must continually strive to deliver better customer service.

The right attitude

Customers evaluate a company on its organizational skills, attitude, appearance, relationships, tools and knowledge. Which is the most important?

Of success, 85% is determined by attitude and only 15% by skills.

Attitude is the key factor in determining our success as a company or as an individual. Eighty-five per cent of success is determined by attitude and only 15% by skills. That tells you something very important about people skills. The adjectives most likely used to describe a successful person or company will be those that describe attitude, not necessarily skills.

Don't take a customer's anger personally, since the customer is angry at a problem, a circumstance, a situation or solution, not at you. Accept the fact that some people are that way. Silence is a good tool. When a customer is irate, start writing down the details of their problem, as this makes them slow down and organize their thoughts.

Why customers react

Losing your temper indicates lack of control. Customers who are angry, aggressive, even nervous, behave that way because they:

- Misunderstand important details or facts
- Lack information about services or policies
- Are frustrated from being left on hold too long
- Are frustrated about an unresolved problem
- Feel they have been wronged or misled
- Have technical problems
- Have stress at work or at home

Other customers may be dissatisfied for these same reasons, but they do not show their dissatisfaction or anger. When you realize that customers act as they do for a whole variety of reasons, you will be less likely to take their feelings or actions personally or to respond emotionally. By understanding your customers, you can provide them with the level of customer service that they expect.

Tips for handling difficult customers

1   *Listen* – Say nothing until the customer has stated his or her grievance. Do not interrupt.

2   *Empathize and apologize* – The customer wants attention and respect, so give it. There need be no loss of dignity in showing empathy and respect to a disappointed, frustrated customer. Making a formal and sincere apology will help to calm and regain a customer's trust.

3   *Establish the reason why the customer is angry* – Is the company at fault? Is the product wrong? Have the company personnel offended the customer? Whether or not the complaint is justified, obtaining precise information is essential.

4   *Give the customer your name* – Give the customer your commitment to resolving his or her problem. Personal attention to a customer's needs cements good customer relations. It also repairs a relationship that has been disrupted.

5   *Follow up the action if any delay is scheduled* – It is necessary to make sure that promises and commitments are met. When staff cannot satisfy an angry customer, even though the standard procedure has been followed, it is time to call in management for help.

6   *Call on management for help with customers who stay angry* – Remember that coping with irate customers is all in a day's work. Understand that the way you handle that particular customer will make the difference in how that customer views the company. Always remain calm, warm, friendly, and genuine; try to solve their problem.

The key steps

1   Learn how to listen to the customer.
2   Learn to hear customers out and to empathize.
3   Defuse the customer's anger with phrases like 'I understand, I see'.
4   Use phrases like 'Thank you for calling'.
5   Always lower your voice when talking to customers who are upset.
6   Don't take a customer's anger personally.

7   If, after using these steps, the customer is still dissatisfied, refer them to your immediate supervisor or your department manager.

MOMENTS OF TRUTH

'Customer satisfaction and motivated employees are the key elements on every company's balance sheet. We used to fly aeroplanes, we had to learn how to fly people.' – Jan Carlzon, former President and CEO of the airline SAS and the author of *Moments of Truth*.

What makes a satisfied customer? According to Carlzon, each customer is likely to meet five employees. SAS flies around 20 million people each year and that makes 100 million 'moments of truth' or contacts that can make or break a relationship. Trying to manage those 100 million moments of truth is a major task that requires considerable delegation of responsibility and authority.

Carlzon believes that getting staff to take the initiative requires a major change in organizational culture. Traditionally, staff were instructed to respond in specific ways to customers. But if the customer behaved in an unpredictable way, staff would have been powerless to help. Only by empowering staff to make decisions and take appropriate action can an organization be truly customer-focused.

Treat customers as individuals

Good people, according to Carlzon, treat customers as individuals and technology can help them do that. Carlzon illustrated the benefits of the approach by citing the example of the business customer who left his ticket at the hotel. An SAS receptionist arranged to collect the ticket and forward it to the customer. The cost was $20, difficult to justify for every customer, but the potential lifetime value of that customer was around $160 000, a worthwhile investment at the moment of truth. How many organizations, he asks, would be prepared to support their front-line staff in that way?

Part of the process is knowing what that customer wants. Technology allows you to build up information on customers and use it to treat them as individuals. Every customer, Carlzon believes, has lifetime value. A young inexperienced business traveller who would not normally receive special treatment has the potential to offer another 35 years' worth of business. It is therefore important to record and use that customer's buying patterns and preferences from the outset.

Customer satisfaction is critical

Customer satisfaction has become increasingly important in every business sector. The head of a leading US manufacturing company explained how he had originally built profitability through cutting costs and increasing profitability. The strategy worked to begin with, but then profits fell. But when that company focused on productivity and service, the situation improved. The company now measures business performance on three factors – customer satisfaction, employee motivation, cash flow. Customer satisfaction and motivated employees are the key elements on the company's balance sheet.

Carlzon concludes, 'In the 80s, we saw a customer in every individual. In the future, we have to learn to see an individual in each customer.'

COMPETENCE SELF-ASSESSMENT

1 How would you rate your customer service skills and those of your staff?
2 Describe the important aspects of listening to customers.
3 What are the top customer complaints about your organization? How would you remedy them?
4 Identify the main customer contact points in your organization.
5 Prepare a 'customer service' job description for the key members of your staff.
6 How do your staff perform against the telephone response checklist?
7 Identify the most important 'moments of truth' in your relationship with customers.
8 Describe the information you would need to be able to treat customers as individuals.
9 How does customer satisfaction relate to the balance sheet?
10 Prepare a personal development programme for your customer-facing staff.

15 Enhancing customer service skills with technology

While effective personal skills are essential in meeting customer needs, technology can help to enhance those skills even further. Telecommunications, in particular, is making an important contribution to quality customer service.

MAKE MORE USE OF THE TELEPHONE

According to the Institute of Direct Marketing, telemarketing is twice as effective as direct mail and inclusion of a telephone number can increase response by up to 185%. The Henley Centre's Telebusiness Survey reports that 'consumers are becoming more and more aware of the benefits of doing business by phone and up to 80% see it as both convenient and easy'.

Telemarketing involves a systematic approach where the telephone is used as a tool for implementing sales and marketing strategies. It can be used to improve the following functions:

Order taking

- Improves speed and accuracy
- More convenient than filling in and posting forms
- Fax or interactive voice means orders can be handled round the clock

New marketing channels

- Opportunities for 'direct' sales
- Reduces administration costs
- Bypasses traditional distribution routes

Market research

- Market research interviews
- Database information from helplines, enquiries, telesales

Market testing

- Opportunity to evaluate different marketing/promotional routes
- Telephone research

International marketing

- Supports round-the-clock marketing
- International freephone numbers available

Sales support

- Following up sales leads
- Qualifying prospects
- Setting up appointments
- Increases salesforce productivity

Outbound selling

- Warm calling qualified prospects

Helplines

- Make expertise available to customers
- Handle minor technical problems

- Reduce customer downtime
- Opportunity for customers to report problems and complaints
- Convenient route demonstrates customer care

Courtesy calls

- Add personal touch to the sales process
- Opportunity to offer additional products and services
- Overcome any initial problems

IMPROVE TELEPHONE RESPONSE

Answering the phone on the third ring may mean 'customer service' to some companies, but what happens if the caller can't reach the right person? New developments in telecommunications can ensure that the caller will always get a response.

One major company found that, on an average day, 10% of their 900 staff would for various reasons be away from their desks. They decided to implement 'hot desking', with staff sharing desks and work areas as necessary. The problem was – how to ensure that customer calls got through to the right people?

New telecommunications techniques mean that telephone calls can be managed via a desktop personal computer, allowing staff to work at any location without affecting communications. Calls can be routed to any desk, to voicemail or to a paging system. This ensures optimum use of space and enhances caller service.

Flexible working practices

This level of flexibility is important to companies who are utilizing new working practices such as team working, work groups, use of external contractors/ specialists and part-time working. These changes in working practice have far-reaching implications for internal and external communications and customer service. Companies have to provide all their users with access to effective communications, wherever and whenever they need them. When customers ask for a named individual they must be sure of making contact quickly and easily.

Keeping in touch with the salesforce

Flexible, effective communications are also essential to the success of the salesforce, who might visit their office only once a week. They need to maintain high levels of contact at all times to ensure the right level of customer service. To reach an individual representative, customers can now call just one number and the call is automatically routed to the most appropriate destination. Calls can be routed to car phones, a secretary, voicemail, the representative's home or the sales support team. If the first choice is unavailable or doesn't answer, automatic call management tries alternative destinations so that no call goes unanswered.

Location-independent working

If staff need the flexibility to move freely around a site or if they do not have a permanent desk, call routing is no longer a problem. Staff who work from home or who travel frequently can also be reached easily. It is also vital to maintain contact when staff are working off-site. Even with mobile telephones, communications can still be difficult. New technology increases the number of options available for call handling and message management. Users can arrange to have calls diverted to colleagues, routed to mobile phones, pagers or home numbers, or stored in voicemail.

Team calls

Many organizations are bringing their people together in teams or work groups to focus the right skills on a specific project or on a service such as accounts, customer service or sales. Call routing improves the efficiency of internal and external communications by ensuring that all calls will be answered, whether individual team members are on-site or not. For example, a 'team call' facility, where the phone number relates to the service instead of a named individual, means callers can be routed to the most suitable member of the team. Team members' calls are routed to their current location, irrespective of where they are working. This allows teams to be split across sites or to work from home and there is no limit to team size.

Improving the quality of communications
No calls are lost.
People are more accessible.
Calls can be automatically routed to the right 'service area', rather than named individuals.
Callers get a quicker response.

PROFITING FROM CUSTOMER CALLS

'If you make it easy for customers to contact you, you'll soon develop closer relationships but put barriers in their way, and they'll just try the next number on their list.' According to the marketing director of a mail order company, the telephone is proving to be a vital element in quality customer service.

If your business receives a high volume of incoming calls – sales, information or service queries, bookings or transaction processing – you need to ensure that those calls are answered quickly and efficiently. A quality response not only enhances customer service, it is the key to increased revenue and profit.

Developments in telecommunications technology mean that sophisticated response systems are no longer the preserve of large corporations. Systems are now available to small and medium-sized businesses that can transform the quality of customer response. The key is call centres, as this telecommunications consultant explains.

'By concentrating your telephone specialists in call centres, supervising their performance, and using a technique known as Automatic Call Distribution (ACD), you can ensure that calls are answered quickly and efficiently, with the optimum use of staff time and telephone lines.'

Call handling in an engineering company

A small engineering company recently invested in a call centre system to handle sales order processing and provide customers with a technical helpline service. Although they had offered telephone support in the past, the service had been hampered by poor call-handling techniques. At peak times, customers would wait several minutes to get through and were sometimes transferred to extensions that were unmanned. The customer's perception was shaped by the call response, not by the service that was eventually delivered.

The system they installed uses a range of computerized tools to monitor performance and improve control over call response. Information on the status of telephone lines and groups of call centre staff shows what is happening to calls as they come in and allows the supervisor to manage operations efficiently. The system also includes features such as call queuing and call prioritization to ensure that the call centre operates cost-effectively and delivers high levels of customer satisfaction.

The engineering company found that the system enabled them to handle the same volume of calls more efficiently but, more important, it allowed them to keep customers informed even while they were waiting. User-friendly queuing techniques are used to ensure that calls are answered in sequence and no calls go unanswered. All incoming calls are queued and answered in order and the system can be programmed to feed calls to waiting or specified agents automatically.

- Calls are automatically routed to the longest waiting agent in a group.
- If all agents in a group are busy, calls can overflow to a second group.
- Calls can be routed to other groups after a preset ringing time.

Enhancing call response

A range of call-processing options can be utilized to enhance call response even further:

- Integral call sequencing reduces the risk that callers will hang up by giving an informative message.
- Voicemail allows callers to leave messages for agents who are unavailable.
- Automated Attendant answers calls automatically and transfers them to the right extension.
- Integrated Voice Response (IVR) order processing system answers callers automatically and takes details without agent intervention.

When call centres are appropriate

You may already have a call centre in your organization but if not, look closely at your business to see if there are opportunities to improve the speed and quality of call response. Call centres are particularly appropriate for the following activities:

- Enquiry and help desks
- Telemarketing
- Financial services
- Retail or wholesale order entry
- Reservation systems
- Customer service departments

By monitoring the length of time it takes for incoming calls to be answered and assessing the workload on different members of staff you can plan a call centre that meets your business needs. These are some of the important factors to consider. What type of calls should the centre handle – orders, enquiries, help, service? Should it be a central facility or based in different regions? What is the target call response time – how long can you keep callers waiting? How many staff and how many lines will be needed to handle planned volumes within the target response times?

Networking facilities allow multi-site companies to operate a single call centre; customers call their local branch, but the call is redirected automatically to the call centre. A distributed call centre network means that callers can overflow to remote sites in peak periods or be diverted to specialist centres of excellence in different sites.

These network options increase flexibility and can be used to enhance customer service even further. Many systems allow you to link computer and business applications to your telephone operations. For example, the integration of screen-based customer information can help to improve productivity and customer service on call response. To maximize the benefits of the call centre, agents can make outbound sales calls or enquiries when incoming traffic is low. For increased productivity, outbound calls can be generated from a database with integrated call information available on screen.

Although the use of call-handling systems is not new, the technology is now more accessible and it is being increasingly used by small and medium-sized organizations in the public and private sector. It can provide the basis for a highly efficient telephone-based customer contact system and research shows that effective contact is a key factor in achieving the highest levels of customer satisfaction.

SETTING UP A CALL CENTRE

If you make it easy for customers to contact you, you'll soon develop closer relationships but put barriers in their way, and they'll just try the next number on their list. If your business receives a high volume of incoming calls – sales, information or service queries, bookings or transaction processing – you need to ensure that those calls are answered quickly and efficiently.

A paging operator uses a call centre solution to answer 4000 calls per hour. Ninety-eight per cent of calls are answered within 8 seconds and only two callers in every thousand hang up before the call is answered.

A security company used a call centre to improve service standards. Service engineers can now access the Shorrock's computer system directly from any standard telephone line. The company was able to double its business without any increase in telephone staff.

A management consultancy implemented a call centre to improve the service available from their IT help desk. This now allows 50% of calls to be handled automatically, and ensures that callers who do need personal attention are answered quickly and efficiently.

Telecommunications systems are now available to small and medium-sized businesses that can transform the quality of customer response. In planning your system, the following are some of the important factors to consider:

- What type of calls should the centre handle – orders, enquiries, help, service?
- Should it be a central facility or based in different regions?
- What is the target call response time – how long can you keep callers waiting?
- How many staff and how many lines will be needed to handle planned volumes within the target response times?

If you are planning to set up your own call centre, the following are the costs you could incur:

- Equipment
- Recruitment of specialist staff
- Training
- Computer support services

Before investing in a fully equipped call centre it may be more effective to operate a pilot programme and carry out cost-benefit analysis. To achieve this you can either:

- Use the services of a telemarketing agency or
- Set up a small-scale operation, possibly using second-user equipment.

HELPLINES KEEP THE CUSTOMERS TALKING

If you've been through the traumas of buying a personal computer, you'll understand the problems of trying to choose from hundreds of 'me-too' products, each one claiming to offer the ultimate solution to your needs. If you then tried to work out which of the manufacturers' extensive hardware/software packages was right for you, you'll understand why customers sometimes need help in choosing a product.

Pre-sales advice builds trust and loyalty

The right advice before a sale can demonstrate customer service from the outset and win loyal customers. That's why increasing numbers of computer companies provide customers and prospects with a freephone helpline and encourage them to talk. Here's how they make the most of the phone.

- The freephone facility encourages people to use the service and discuss their requirements at length.
- The helplines are manned by specialists who combine technical knowledge with an ability to talk to individuals at the right level – callers are not intimidated by talking to people who reply in jargon.
- Helpline staff talk about the customer's needs – how do you plan to use the computer, what results do you want, how often do you use it? They concentrate on identifying the customer's needs, not doing a sales pitch on their products.
- Staff are encouraged to develop a relationship over the phone, not deal with queries as quickly as possible and meet a daily target. Dialogue and a relaxed attitude help to build customer confidence.

The customer who gets honest, straightforward answers will trust the company. In a commodity market, that level of customer service can be an important differentiator.

So, don't just reserve helplines for operating problems or service requests. Use them to build a relationship before the selling starts. Once you have established customer needs, your sales team can concentrate on offering the right product. The result – customer satisfaction at every stage.

SETTING UP A HELPLINE

Giving your customers advice and guidance over a helpline can demonstrate customer service and improve customer satisfaction. That's why increasing numbers of companies provide customers and prospects with a helpline and encourage them to use it. In practice, a departmental helpline is likely to be manned by a single person, but the same principles apply.

- The helplines are manned by specialists who combine technical knowledge with an ability to talk to individuals at the right level – callers are not intimidated by talking to people who reply in jargon.
- Helpline staff talk about the customer's needs – what problems do you have?

■ Staff are encouraged to develop a relationship over the phone, not deal with queries as quickly as possible and meet a daily target. Dialogue and a relaxed attitude help to build customer confidence.

Guidelines for a customer query helpline

■ Determine the scope of the service.
■ Set opening times to suit customer-calling patterns.
■ Use staff with up-to-date knowledge of company policies and products.
■ Train staff in customer service techniques to ensure that they can deal effectively with people who may not be familiar with your products.
■ Provide staff with lists of contacts for specific types of information.
■ Provide staff with access to any relevant databases.
■ Deal with queries immediately, where possible, or arrange to call back the customer on more complex queries.
■ Check that customer has received any 'call backs' within the agreed timescale.
■ Make a follow-up call to ensure that the customer is satisfied with the response.

Guidelines for a customer complaint helpline

■ Make it easy and convenient for customers to complain.
■ Set opening times to suit customer calling patterns.
■ Use staff with up-to-date knowledge of policies and procedures.
■ Find out what the complainant wants – it may be an explanation, compensation, an apology or simply an opportunity to let off steam.
■ Train staff in customer service techniques to ensure that they can deal effectively with people who may be angry or difficult.
■ Provide staff with guidelines on the actions they can take to deal with different types of complaint.
■ Provide staff with access to relevant databases.
■ Provide staff with lists of contacts for authorization of different types of response.

- Deal with complaints immediately, where possible, or arrange to call back the customer where further information/authorization is required.
- Operate an escalation procedure to deal with complaints which cannot be resolved within agreed timescales.
- Check that customer has received any 'call backs' within the agreed timescale.
- Make a follow-up call to ensure that the customer is satisfied with the response.
- Record details of all complaints and pass information to the management team for improvement action.

Determining helpline staffing levels

This section is more appropriate to organizations handling larger numbers of helpline calls, but the principle of ensuring that calls are handled within a reasonable time applies, whatever the size of the helpline.

- Ask your telephone/network supplier to provide a report on the number of calls to the helpline number.
- Determine the current/planned level of calls per day.
- Ask your telephone/network supplier to provide a report on the average waiting time for calls to the helpline number.
- Assess whether the average time meets, exceeds or fails to meet the target time.
- Decide how many helpline staff do you currently/plan to use.
- Work out the ratio of staff to calls.
- Analyse the pattern of calls during the day/week/month/year, using reports from your telephone/network supplier. Identify the peaks and troughs.
- Assess the number of staff required at peak and off-peak periods.
- Decide whether you can meet target staffing levels from current resources.
- Assess the potential benefit of using technologies such as voicemail to handle some of the incoming calls.

Developing helpline skills

- Assess the skills required for different types of helpline service.

- Review the current skills of your helpline staff:
  - Knowledge of legislation
  - Knowledge of company procedures
  - Telephone technique
  - Customer service skills.
- Compare the current skills profile with the skills requirement.
- Identify the skills that need to be improved.
- Consider using specialists to support helpline staff.
- Obtain customer feedback to evaluate staff performance.
- If you introduce new helpline technology, ensure that staff are trained in using the new technology.

Customer information for helplines

- Provide staff with customer information to ensure prompt response and personal service.
- Obtain information from existing staff records.
- Check and update information each time a customer calls.
- Provide information in an easy-to-use format, ideally on a personal computer screen.
- Use a simple code to access information quickly, for example name, department, post code.

Helpline escalation procedures

A problem may need to be 'escalated' to a higher level if it cannot be resolved by helpline staff within an agreed period of time.

- Set target response times.
- Appoint a supervisor/manager with responsibility for monitoring conformance to target response times.
- Escalate any queries that exceed target times to designated manager.
- Monitor response to escalated query.
- If necessary, escalate query to senior management/director level to ensure resources are focused on successful resolution.

Monitoring helpline performance: sample questionnaire

Name
Department   Extension

1 How often do you use the helpline?
   - more than once a week, monthly, occasionally

2 When did you last call the helpline?
   - date, day, time of day
3 What was the nature of your call?
4 How long did we take to answer your call?
   - 3 rings, 6–10 rings, longer
5 If your call was held in a queue, how long were you kept
   waiting?
   - less than 1 minute, 1–2 minutes, longer
6 Did you feel the waiting time was:
   - brief, satisfactory, too long
7 Were you kept informed of your progress in the queue?
8 Did the staff treat you courteously?
9 Did the staff check that your details were up to date?
10 Were the staff able to deal with your query immediately?
11 If not, were you given a specific time when someone would
    call you back?
12 Did someone call you back within the agreed time limit?
13 Do you consider the call-back period:
    - brief, satisfactory, too long
14 How do you rate our helpline staff in the following areas:
    - professional knowledge, ability to provide advice at the
    right level, efficiency in dealing with your call
15 Do you have any specific concerns or comments about the
    helpline service?

MOBILE COMMUNICATIONS IMPROVE RESPONSE, EFFICIENCY AND CUSTOMER SERVICE

Mobile communications, such as radio, telephone or data communications systems, can add an extra dimension to your service performance. By keeping in constant touch and supporting your field staff with up-to-date information, you can ensure that they provide customers with the highest standards of service.

Mobile communications solutions

Mobile radio	Mobile data
Wide-area paging	On-site paging
Cellular telephony	

Your field staff can respond to customer requests in the shortest possible time, reassure customers that help is on the way and update them on urgent deliveries. Customers have the peace of mind that delay will be minimal and they know they can rely on you for a prompt, quality response every time. That level of customer service is vital for companies who offer service, repair, distribution or security services.

You can guarantee the fastest response times to a call-out, speed up distribution, ensure that vital replacement parts are there when they are needed and retain customer loyalty with an efficient, professional service. Because you are in constant contact, you can prioritize work and ensure that your resources are concentrated on supporting your key accounts.

Mobile data communications can improve your competitiveness even further. You can transmit messages or important customer and service information such as stock availability and part numbers, even when the driver is away from the vehicle. You can also support efficient operating procedures such as daily work schedules, confirmation of arrival times or job completion to improve control and efficiency. Service records can be quickly and easily updated as soon as a job is completed and invoices or receipts can be transmitted to the field to improve cashflow.

Mobile voice and data communications can also help you to make the most efficient and productive use of your resources. You can save on journey times and fuel costs by avoiding cancelled calls and you can easily re-arrange call allocations to take account of changing traffic conditions, urgent requests or other problems. You can also ensure that your field staff are meeting their schedules and improve overall control of your resources.

LAPTOPS PROVIDE MOBILE DESIGN SERVICE

A security company has equipped its field support team with laptop computers and a software package that allows them to design a simple security system on the spot. The surveyor measures the customer's premises and feeds in details of the security requirements. The program can then provide an accurate, comprehensive specification and quotation, and a practical action plan that can be implemented quickly and cost effectively.

This enables a surveyor to design and estimate a project on-site, quickly and accurately, giving the customer an immediate indication of cost and timescale. The information can be transferred by modem to the company's head office where a printed quotation is generated and the information stored on a database for use in the project.

Before the introduction of the system, the design and estimate would have been prepared back at the office. The process would not have started until the surveyor returned to the office with the details and it could have been further delayed by current workload.

The company believes that this helps them to win business through a combination of speedy response and customer service that cannot be matched by traditional methods.

KEEPING IN CONTACT WITH KEY STAFF

Do your customers have problems contacting key members of staff? If they're on the move and frequently away from the office, this can be a serious problem. When customers can't get through, customer service goes down and you could be losing business.

Cellnet, the mobile communications company, has introduced a product called Personal Assistant which helps staff to be fully contactable, even when they're on the move. As part of the product development process, the company carried out a survey into the views of executives. The main conclusions were as follows:

- 68% of those interviewed worry about loss of business because they are out of touch with base, or because customers cannot reach them on time.
- 55% feel that there is too little time to meet every commitment and admit that they do not handle their messages as effectively as they could.
- 49% estimate that they are away from the office for the equivalent of a whole working day each week.
- 10% estimate that they are away for more than 30 hours each week.

In those circumstances, it is important to improve the level of contact. The Cellnet Personal Assistant provides a range of key communications services:

- *Single number* – The number never changes whether it is office phone, home phone, mobile phone, fax, or modem. Callers do not have to remember a string of numbers.
- *Find-me facility* – This takes the callers through series of pre-programmed numbers automatically to reach their contact at the current location. Callers can also select voicemail if they just want to leave a message.
- *Call screening* – The user is advised of the caller's number and has the option of taking the call immediately or routing it to voicemail.
- *Voicemail* – Callers are automatically routed to voicemail whenever the number is engaged or the user is unavailable.
- *Fax store/forward* – Faxes can be stored or sent forward immediately to the most convenient number.
- *Notification* – The system alerts users that they have a message or fax waiting.

A system like this makes it easy for staff on the move to improve their efficiency and ensure that customers can always contact them.

COMPETENCE SELF-ASSESSMENT

1 Describe the departmental functions which could be improved through better use of the telephone.
2 How important are flexible working practices to your department or organization?
3 How would you use automatic call distribution within your department?
4 Describe how you would use a call centre.
5 Prepare a plan for introducing helpline services.
6 Describe the scope of your helpline services.
7 Prepare a plan for training helpline staff.
8 How would you utilize mobile data communications?
9 How would you use laptop computers to improve customer service?
10 What are your priorities in customer service technology?

16 Dealing with customer service problems

Customers who have their complaints resolved are likely to remain loyal and tell friends and colleagues how their complaints have been handled. But what happens to the rest? Do they complain with their feet? Do they remain silently resentful or do they tell their friends about the bad service they have endured? Complaints are vital to a customer-focused company. They highlight weaknesses in customer service, identify areas for improvement and provide an opportunity to demonstrate high levels of customer care.

ENCOURAGING COMPLAINTS

How can you make the most of complaints?

- Encourage customers to complain – put up signs, provide addresses or phone numbers on all customer communications.
- Make it easy for customers to complain by providing a freephone number or freepost address and giving customers a named contact.

- Make sure that the nominated phone line is manned by someone experienced in customer-handling skills.
- Give the contact the authority to resolve complaints and, if necessary, to provide reasonable compensation.
- Ensure that an escalation process is in position to deal with complaints that cannot be resolved immediately.
- Thank the customer for highlighting the problem and allowing the company to resolve it.
- Assure customers that remedial action will be taken.
- Set up a process for recording and analysing complaints.

A positive attitude to complaints can bring its rewards. The financial performance of Marks & Spencer, for example, has not suffered as a result of their commitment to settling complaints without fuss.

PAYING THE PRICE FOR CUSTOMER SERVICE

A high street bank has just told its customers that it will pay them if it makes a mistake. The bank has published a charter which sets out its standards for service. The charter covers the following points:

- It will not make errors on statements.
- It will set up and pay standing orders without mistakes.
- It will automatically issue cheque books and cards to ensure that customers always have them when they need them.
- They will give decisions on overdrafts and personal loans immediately and have funds available within an hour of agreement.
- They will open new accounts within 48 hours of application.

If the bank makes a mistake on any of those points, the customer will receive £10.

A leading health insurance company offers an equally flexible approach. They promise their corporate customers that if they fail to meet standards or miss deadlines, they will pay compensation. For example, for a delay in issuing settlement cheques, the company pays £5, but if it fails to notify customers of renewal dates 3 weeks in advance, they pay £100.

The gesture is worth more than the money

The company reports that its corporate clients are not specifically interested in the money itself, but they appreciate that the gesture demonstrates the company's commitment to quality customer service. Demonstrating commitment in this way shows customers that you are serious about your standards.

The following are some of the actions you can take to implement a customer service payment system in your organization:

- Identify the factors that customers feel most strongly about.
- Set customer performance standards for each factor.
- Introduce training programmes to ensure high levels of performance.
- Tell customers about the standards and explain the methods of compensation.
- Measure performance.

LEARNING FROM COMPLAINTS

Although an effective complaints-handling procedure is important, it is also essential to use complaints as a form of research that enables you to improve your standards of service and your processes. To make the most of customer complaints, set up a process for recording, analysing and taking action.

- Ensure that all complaints are recorded; where possible, include the name of the person, the date, time and a summary of the complaint and the response.
- Identify the source of the complaint and assess whether corrective action is needed.
- Monitor the frequency of different types of complaint to set priorities for action programmes.
- Monitor product and process performance after corrective action has been taken.

Telling customers how to complain

You should cover the following points:

- Your policy on complaints
- How customers can complain
- How you will respond
- Timescales
- The next stage if the complaint cannot be resolved.

REPLYING TO CUSTOMER CONCERNS

Customers expect a prompt and positive response to their complaints. Whether you telephone or write depends on the nature and timing of the problem, but you should take the opportunity to not only deal with the problem, but reassure the customer that you are committed to the highest standards of service. The following is a series of scenarios that you might face:

- Problem with the product
- Poor service quality
- Product no longer available
- Parts delayed
- Product out of guarantee
- Late delivery of product
- Demand for compensation for poor service
- Customer has damaged product
- Product incapable of repair
- Offer of alternative
- Customer wants to make a formal complaint
- Customer/company cannot settle a dispute

Examples of replies

Version 1: Problem now solved

Thank you for letting us know that you are now fully satisfied with ... While we aim to achieve the highest standards from the outset, we understand that problems can occur and we are pleased that you took the trouble to bring it to our attention.

We aim to respond positively to our customers' concerns and we will be looking very closely at the particular ... process that was used. We hope that you would wish to use our services on future occasions and we look forward to dealing with you.

Thank you once again for contacting ...

Version 2: Company unable to contact customer

You recently contacted us about ... problem. I wanted to discuss this with you personally over the telephone, but I have been unable to reach you. If you would like to contact ... (name/number of someone who can take calls for you) and let them know when we can reach you, I will call you back.

I am sorry to hear that you have a problem and I would like to settle the matter as quickly as possible. While we aim to achieve the highest standards from the outset, we understand that problems can occur and we are pleased that you took the trouble to bring it to our attention. We aim to respond positively to our customers' concerns and we will be looking very closely at the particular . . . process that was used.

Thank you once again for contacting . . . and I hope to speak to you very soon.

Version 3: Problem doing the rounds

You recently contacted . . . about . . . problem and I understand that you have not yet had a satisfactory reply. I am sorry that there has been a delay and I am now taking personal responsibility for the matter.
EITHER
I wanted to discuss this with you personally over the telephone, but I have been unable to reach you. If you would like to contact . . . (name/number of someone who can take calls for you) and let them know when we can reach you, I will call you back.
OR
I want to discuss this with you personally over the telephone, and I will be contacting you in the next few days.

I hope that we can then settle the matter as quickly as possible. While we aim to achieve the highest standards from the outset, we understand that problems can occur and we are pleased that you took the trouble to bring it to our attention. We aim to respond positively to our customers' concerns and we will be looking very closely at the particular . . . process that was used.

Thank you once again for contacting . . . and I hope to speak to you very soon.

Version 4: Problem needs specialist reply

You recently contacted . . . about . . . problem and I understand that you have not yet had a satisfactory reply. I am sorry that there has been a delay and I am now taking personal responsibility for the matter.

Your query is being investigated by a specialist in . . . department and I have asked that person to report back to me within . . . days. I will then telephone you to discuss the matter and, if necessary, arrange for the specialist to contact you directly.

I hope that we can then settle the matter as quickly as possible. While we aim to achieve the highest standards from the outset, we understand that problems can occur and we are pleased that you took the trouble to bring it to our attention. We aim to respond positively to our customers' concerns and we will be looking very closely at the particular ... process that was used.

Thank you once again for contacting ... and I hope to speak to you very soon.

DEALING WITH AWKWARD COMPLAINTS

A customer bought a fax machine with a year's guarantee. At the time of purchase, the customer was offered an extended service contract which covered the parts and labour costs of any repairs for the next two years in return for payment of a single premium. The extended service contract included an annual check-up. The fax machine developed a serious fault just one month after the end of the first year guarantee and eventually became unusable. However, the customer had declined the offer of the extended service contract.

Faulty product or customer choice?

The customer returned the unit to the company's service department, claiming that it was faulty. However, the company pointed out that the fault had occurred outside the guarantee period and there was therefore no liability. The company also pointed out that the customer had declined the offer of an extended service contract and had therefore accepted the risk. They explained that the initial second-year check-up would have identified the fault before it became serious.

Standing by a reputation

The customer expressed concern that such a serious fault could occur so soon after the guarantee expired and argued that the company should accept some responsibility for the fault. The company decided to repair the unit at its own cost as a gesture of goodwill.

Avoiding the risk

To prevent such a risk and add value to the product, the company decided to offer a free check-up at the end of the guarantee period. If any faults were identified, the customer would only pay half of the actual cost. The company also took the opportunity to offer the extended service contract and found that a higher percentage of customers now took it up.

This is a proactive form of customer service that can help to prevent misunderstandings and demonstrates a high level of customer care.

WINNING BACK LOST CUSTOMERS

If you lose a customer, do you just treat it as an inevitable event and do nothing? To make sure it does not happen again, you should carry out research into lost accounts and try to identify reasons for the loss. This not only demonstrates good customer service, even though it may be too late, it also helps to identify weaknesses in customer relationships.

- Use an independent research organization to carry out the work.
- Provide the research company with important account information so that they do not waste the customer's time.
- Ensure that the research company explains the purpose of the call, which is not win back the business, but to identify areas for improvement in the service.
- Use the findings of the research to improve areas of weakness.

The following is an example of a letter that can be used as part of the recovery process.

Dear Customer

We were sorry that you have decided that you no longer wish to do business with us. We appreciate that you have very good reasons for changing suppliers and we hope that you are enjoying a satisfactory standard of service from your new supplier.

We always aim to provide the highest standards of service to all our customers, but it may be that, on this occasion, we have failed to do that.

We would therefore be grateful if you would take the time to respond to a telephone call from an independent research company who will be contacting you shortly.

OR

We would be grateful if you could complete the attached questionnaire and return it to the research company in the reply-paid envelope.

We have asked the research company to help us identify any areas of weakness so that we can continue to improve our service. We would like to assure you that the research company will not try to win back your business. Obviously, all information will be treated in the strictest confidence.

We hope that you will be able to cooperate, and we would like to express our appreciation for the opportunity to handle your business in the past.

The letter

The following are some of the key points from the letter:

- Thank the customer for past business.
- Respect the customer's choice of supplier.
- Make the interview/questionnaire as convenient as possible.
- Stress that this is not a sales exercise.

Questionnaire/interview

Your aim is to find out why customers have moved their business to another supplier and to use that information to identify possible areas of weakness in your own standards of service.

Do not ask the customer questions such as

- What type of products were they buying from you?
- How long have they been a customer?
- What was the value of their purchases?

This is information that should be on your records. Asking questions like this will only confirm to the customer that you were not really that interested in the business.

Concentrate on specific questions such as

- Were you dissatisfied with price/delivery/quality or other factors?
- Would you have changed if the company had improved any of those factors?

You may be able to ask questions such as

- What made you choose your new supplier?
- Why do you think the new supplier is better than the previous supplier?

Remember, you are dependent on the cooperation of a customer that has recently 'dropped' your company. It may not be possible to get all the information you want, but you should not push customers who are unwilling to answer certain questions.

COMPETENCE SELF-ASSESSMENT

1 Describe your procedure for handling customer complaints.
2 Do you encourage customer complaints? If not, how would you do this?
3 Describe how you would compensate customers for mistakes.
4 What action do you take when customers have complained?
5 Describe the types of complaints your department has to resolve.
6 Write a letter responding to three common types of complaints.
7 What is your company's policy on warranties?
8 Do you have a policy for winning back lost customers?
9 What are the main reasons for customer defection?
10 Prepare a questionnaire aimed at lost customers.

Conclusion: how well do you meet customer needs?

If you want to measure achievement and improvement in customer service, the only true measure is customer satisfaction from the customer's point of view.

DESIGNING A CUSTOMER-SATISFACTION SURVEY

Two types of survey can be sent to customers who have recently purchased a product or service; the first would be sent after a short interval, say a week or a month after purchase; the second would be sent six months or a year after initial purchase. The first is to establish the customer's response to the sales process, and the second to establish how the customer feels about the product or service in use and how they feel about the aftercare they have received.

There are four key factors in designing your survey:

1   Which activities are you going to measure?
2   Whose performance will you measure?
3   What measures will you use?
4   How frequently will you measure performance?

What to measure

Your questionnaire should cover the aspects of service that are important from a customer's point of view. These might include:

- The response of sales staff
- The location and convenience of the sales outlet
- Convenience of opening hours
- Ease of parking
- Availability of product information
- Product knowledge of staff
- Waiting time to be served
- Choice of payment methods
- Presentation of product
- Availability of finance
- Explanation of aftercare.

These topics help you to assess how satisfied customers are with the sales process. A questionnaire which followed up at six months or a year after purchase would focus on customer satisfaction with the product or service and the quality of after-care. It might cover topics such as:

- The quality and performance of the product
- The reliability of the product
- The benefits of the service
- The standard of the service
- The response to any queries
- The value of any instruction manuals
- The quality of after-care service
- The standard and speed of after-care
- The value of the warranty
- Availability of replacement parts
- Flexibility of service plans
- Availability of accessories.

Who will you measure?

Customer-satisfaction surveys can be used to assess the overall level of customer satisfaction with a company or an individual aspect of service, for example:

- 76% of customers are satisfied with company x.
- 93% of customers are satisfied with the warranty, but only 53% are satisfied with the quality of product information.

It can also be used as a basis for comparing the performance of different groups within a company. These could include:

- Individual customer-facing staff
- Departments
- Product or service groups
- Branches in a network
- Companies within a group.

What measures will you use?

There are two commonly used approaches:

1   Customers to respond to questions such as 'How satisfied are you with . . . ' using a scale of satisfaction – fully satisfied, very satisfied, satisfied, not very satisfied, very dissatisfied.
2   Customers respond to the question using a numerical scale, 'on a scale of 1–10, how satisfied were you with . . .'; 1 is very dissatisfied, 10 is very satisfied.

Customers should also be given space to provide written comments on particular aspects of the service, and, in some cases, ask for specific actions such as an explanation from the departmental manager.

How frequently should you measure?

There is no simple answer to this question, but several factors should be considered:

- How large is your customer base? It may be more practical to survey small groups regularly to monitor performance over a period of time.
- How frequently do customers purchase products and services? Although it may be impractical to measure satisfaction every time, particularly with fast-moving products, regular surveys can highlight changes in performance.
- Are there problems in customer service? Frequent surveys can help you to monitor changes in satisfaction levels after improvement actions have been taken.

Acting on the results

Although the results of the survey may be interesting in themselves, they are only of real value if they are used as the basis for improvement programmes. Low ratings or a decline in satisfaction with particular aspects of service highlights a need for action. Review the results, identify areas for improvement and measure again after you have taken corrective action. You should also publish results internally to customer-facing staff so that they are aware of customer-satisfaction levels.

HOW WELL DO YOU MEET CUSTOMER NEEDS?

'Every client will recommend us.' Is this a pipe dream or a process that can be managed? It is a customer service vision that drives companies and it is the starting point for standards of customer service excellence that every company can achieve.

Research from the automotive industry shows that after-sales service can generate ten times the number of customer contacts as the original sale, so it is vital that every contact with the customer is a quality contact. Customer service excellence is, therefore, an attitude that permeates the whole company, and it suggests that every employee at every level is focused on customer needs, whether they deliver customer service or not.

Achieving customer service excellence is a key objective for every manager. It can ensure that every day-to-day decision, every communication, every business process is focused on customers' real needs. While many companies limit their customer service initiatives to direct customer-facing activities, this book shows that there are a wide variety of actions that can be utilized to improve relations with customers – from making it easier for customers to place orders to developing customized products and services designed specifically for a customer.

Without a commitment to continuous customer service excellence, individual customer service activities will only be short-term fixes. Customer-driven companies profit because they take a long-term view of customer relationships.

Index